Read **AND** Speak

Arabic

Language Pack for Beginners

الهلا

by Jane Wightwick
Mahmoud Gaafar

g-and-W

Published by g-and-w publishing
5 Churchway
Haddenham
Buckinghamshire HP17 8AB
UK

First edition 2004
Second edition 2012
© g-and-w publishing 2004, 2012

ISBN 978-1903103-326

Printed in China
by WKT Co. Ltd.

1 2 3 4 5 6 7 8   19 18 17 16 15 14 13 12

CONTENTS

PLUS...

- 8 tear-out cards for fun games

- Audio CD for listening and speaking practice

- Online activities to enhance learning

Read & Speak   ARABIC

Welcome to *Read & Speak Arabic*. This programme will introduce you to the Arabic language in easy-to-follow steps. The focus is on enjoyment and understanding, on *reading* words rather than writing them yourself. Through activities and games you'll learn how to read and speak basic Arabic in less time than you thought possible.

You'll find these features in your programme:

	Key Words	See them written and hear them on the CD to improve your pronunciation.
	Language Focus	Clear, simple explanations of language points to help you build up phrases for yourself.
?	*Activities*	Practise what you have learnt through reading, listening and speaking activities.
	Games	With tear-out components. Challenge yourself or play with a friend. A great, fun way to review.
	Audio CD	Hear the key words and phrases and take part in interactive listening and speaking activities. You'll find the track numbers next to the activities in your book.

If you want to give yourself extra confidence with reading the script, you will find *The Arabic 100 Word Exercise Book* the ideal pre-course companion to this programme. *The Arabic 100 Word Exercise Book* introduces the Arabic script through 100 key everyday words, many of which also feature in *Read & Speak Arabic*.

So now you can take your first steps in Arabic with confidence, enjoyment and a real sense of progress.

1

Whenever you see the audio CD symbol, you'll find listening and speaking activities on your CD. The symbol shows the track number.	Track 1 is an introduction to the sounds of Arabic. Listen to this before you start and come back to it again at later stages if you need to.

 ## Key Words

2

Look at the script for each key word and try to visualize it, connecting its image to the pronunciation you hear on your CD.

أهلا **ahlan**	*hello*	*Arabic names:*	
مع السلامة **ma'a s-salaama**	*goodbye*	فاطمة **faaTima**[1]	*(female)*
		سمير **sameer**	*(male)*
اسم **ism**	*name*	زينة **zayna**	*(female)*
اسمي **ismee**	*my name*	يوسف **yoosef**	*(male)*

(1) Capital letters in the pronunciation, e.g. **faaTima**, indicate emphatic sounds (refer to page 91 and audio track 1).

Remember that Arabic reads *right to left* and most short vowels (**a, i, u**) are not written as part of the main script. They can be included as marks above and below the letters but you won't normally see them. Refer to the alphabet table on page 90 if you want to work out the individual letters in a word, but try to let this happen gradually as you progress.

Don't expect to take it all in at once. If you find yourself using strategies at first such as recognizing words by their initial letters or shapes, think of this a positive start and not as "cheating".

How do you say it?

Join the script to the pronunciation, as in the example.

ma`a s-salaama	أهلا
ismee	مع السلامة
yoosef	اسم
ism	اسمي
ahlan	فاطمة
faaTima	سمير
zayna	زينة
sameer	يوسف

What does it mean?

Now say the Arabic out loud and write the English next to each.
Remember to start on the *right*.

_____ مع السلامة		_hello_ أهلا
_____ اسم		_____ زينة
_____ فاطمة		_____ اسمي
_____ سمير		_____ يوسف

Language Focus

Most Arabic letters join to the next letter in a word and change their shape to a greater or lesser extent when they join. Six letters do not join, the most common of which is **alif** (ا). The table on page 90 shows how the individual letters change.

As a general principle the left-hand side (or "tail") of a letter is removed before the following letter is joined.

Look at how these words you have met are formed (read *right to left*):

ma'a مع = ع + م

ism اسم = م + س + ا

sameer سمير = ر + ي + م + س

zayna زينة = ة + ن + ي + ز

My name in Arabic is made up of the word اسم (**ism**) meaning *name* and the ending ـي (**-ee**) meaning *my*. Notice when you join the ending, the tail of the م (**m**) is taken off: اسمي (**ismee**). You can also add the word أنا (**ana**), meaning *I*, to the front of the phrase:

(أنا) اسمي... (**ana**) **ismee...** *My name is...*

There is no equivalent of *is*, so to make a sentence all you have to do is to add your own name:

(أنا) اسمي سمير. (**ana**) **ismee sameer.** *My name is Sameer.*

When you address someone you already know by their name, you can put يا (**yaa**) in front of their name:

أهلا يا زينة. **ahlan yaa zayna.** *Hello, Zayna.*

أهلا يا يوسف. **ahlan yaa yoosef.** *Hello, Yoosef.*

Practise introducing yourself and learn some useful replies on your CD.

3

What are they saying?

Write the correct number in the word balloons.

١ أهلا، أنا اسمي فاطمة.
ahlan, ana ismee faaTima.

٢ أهلا يا سمير.
ahlan yaa sameer.

٣ مع السلامة!
ma`a s-salaama.

٤ أهلا يا زينة
ahlan yaa zayna.

What do you hear?

Work out the phrases below. Then listen and tick (✔)
the two phrases you hear on your audio CD.

4

١ مع السلامة يا فاطمة! ☐

٢ أنا اسمي سمير. ☐

٣ مع السلامة يا يوسف! ☐

٤ أهلا يا زينة. ☐

٥ أهلا! ☐

Key Words

5

ما؟ **maa?**	*what (is)?*	صباح **SabaaH**	*morning*
اسمك **ismak** *(feminine:* **ismik***)*	*your name*	مساء **masaa'**	*evening*
من فضلك **min faDlak** *(feminine:* **min faDlik***)*	*please*	صباح الخير **sabaaH al-khayr**	*good morning*
شكرا **shukran**	*thank you*	مساء الخير **masaa' al-khayr**	*good evening*

Language Focus

You already know how to say *name* – اسم (**ism**) and *my name* – اسمي (**ismee**). To say *your name* you need to add the ending ك : اسمك (**ismak**). The pronunciation changes to **ismik** when referring to a female, but the Arabic spelling remains the same. The same is true with the phrase من فضلك, *please*, which literally means "from your favour", and is pronounced **min faDlak** when talking to a male, but **min faDlik** when talking to a female.

To ask someone their name, add ما (**maa**), *what,* in front of اسمك (**ismak/ismik**):

ما اسمك؟ **maa ismak?**
What's your name? (to a male)

اسمي سمير. **ismee sameer.**
My name's Sameer.

ما اسمك؟ **maa ismik?**
What's your name? (to a female)

أنا اسمي فاطمة. **ana ismee faaTima.** *My name's Fatima.*

At the conference

You are registering your name at a conference.
Take part in the conversation on your CD with the receptionist.

6

What does it mean?

Match the English word balloons to the Arabic.

For example: **1d**

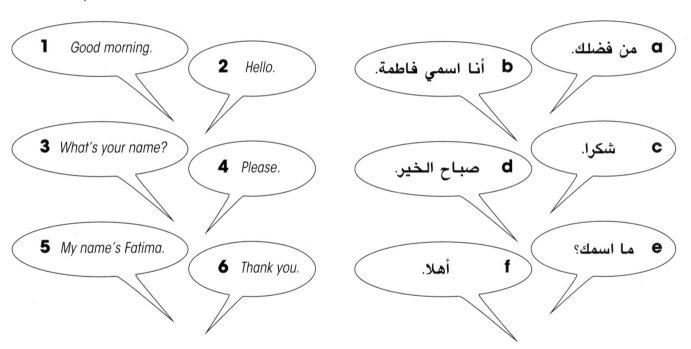

1 Good morning.

2 Hello.

3 What's your name?

4 Please.

5 My name's Fatima.

6 Thank you.

a من فضلك.

b أنا اسمي فاطمة.

c شكرا.

d صباح الخير.

e ما اسمك؟

f أهلا.

Which word?

Write the correct number of the word in the box
to complete the conversation, as in the example.
(Don't forget, read *right to left*.)

_____ 2 ___ الخير.

أهلا. مساء _____.

أنا _____ يوسف. _____ اسمك؟

اسمي _____.

2 مساء		1 اسمي	
5 الخير	4 زينة	3 ما	

Language Focus

The most common way of saying *Mr.* is using الأستاذ (**al-ustaaᴛʜ**) in front of either the first or the second name: الأستاذ علي (**al-ustaaᴛʜ 'alee**); الأستاذ الحلبي (**al-ustaaᴛʜ al-Halabee**). *Mrs.* or *Ms.* is most commonly مدام (**madaam**): مدام زينة (**madaam zayna**). *Miss* is الآنسة (**al-aanisa**), usually used with the first name: الآنسة فاطمة (**al-aanisa faaTima**).

English names with an Arabic pronunciation twist can sound a bit different. Vowels tend to be long to distinguish them from Arabic words, so *Harry* becomes **haari** (هاري). Arabic also doesn't have the sound "*p*", so "*b*" is usually substituted: *Peter* becomes **beetar** (بيتر) and *Penny* becomes **bini** (بني). Consonant clusters (groups of consonants together) are alien to the Arab ear, turning names like *Charles* into **tishaarliz** (تشارلز).

What are their names?

Can you work out these English names written in Arabic script?
Use the alphabet table on page 90 to help you if you want.

_____	جاين	*Suzanne*	سوزان
_____	نانسي	_____	توني
_____	مارك	_____	لوسي
_____	ماري	_____	سام

In or out?

Who is in the office today and who is out at meetings? Look at the wallchart and write the names in English in the correct column, as in the example.

مارك	✔
زينة	✔
هاري	✘
سمير	✔
لوسي	✘
فاطمة	✘
سام	✔
تشارلز	✔
جاين	✘
يوسف	✔

IN

Mark

OUT

The Name Game

1. Tear out Game Card 1 at the back of your book and cut out the name cards (leave the sentence-build cards at the bottom of the sheet for the moment).

2. Put the cards Arabic side up and see if you can recognize the names. Turn over the cards to see if you were correct.

3. Keep shuffling the cards and testing yourself until you can read all the names.

4. Then cut out the extra sentence-build cards at the bottom of the sheet and make mini-dialogues. For example:

– sabaaH al-khayr. maa ismak?

– ahlan. ismee sameer.

5. You can also play with a friend. Make mini-dialogues for each other to read. If you both have a book, you can play Pairs (pelmanism) with both sets of sentence-build cards, saying the words as you turn over the cards.

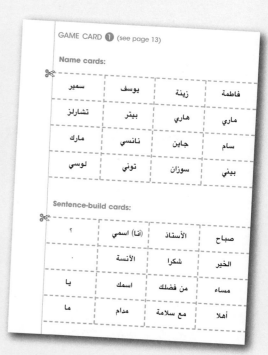

GAME CARD 1 (see page 13)

Name cards:

فاطمة	زينة	يوسف	سمير
ماري	هاري	بيتر	تشارلز
سام	جاين	نانسي	مارك
بيني	سوزان	توني	لوسي

Sentence-build cards:

صباح	الأستاذ	(أنا) اسمي	؟
الخير	شكرا	الآنسة	.
مساء	من فضلك	اسمك	يا
أهلا	مع سلامة	مدام	ما

 Key Words

7

	مصر	miSr	Egypt		بريطانيا	biriTaanya	Britain
	العراق	al-ʿiraaq	Iraq		كندا	kanada	Canada
	سوريا	sooriya	Syria		إيرلندا	eerlanda	Ireland
	أمريكا	amreeka	America		أستراليا	usturalya	Australia
	بلد	balad	country		مدينة	madeena	city

Notice that when an Arabic word starts with a vowel, this is written with an **alif** (ا), often with a small symbol called a **hamza** above (أ), or below (إ) if the word starts with **i** or **ee**.

To learn new words, try covering the English and looking at the Arabic script and pronunciation. Start from the first word and work your way to the last word seeing if you can remember the English.

Then do the same but this time starting from the bottom and moving up to the first word. See if you can go down and up three times without making any mistakes. Then try looking only at the Arabic script. When you can recognize all the words, cover the Arabic and this time look at the English saying the Arabic out loud.

Where are the countries?

Write the number next to the country, as in the example.

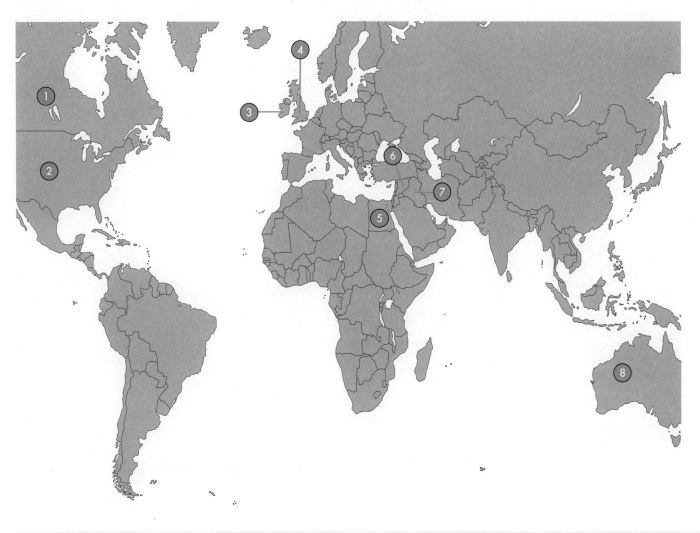

مصر ____	أستراليا ____	إيرلندا ____	أمريكا 2
كندا ____	بريطانيا ____	سوريا ____	العراق ____

How do you say it?

Join the English to the pronunciation and the Arabic script, as in the example.

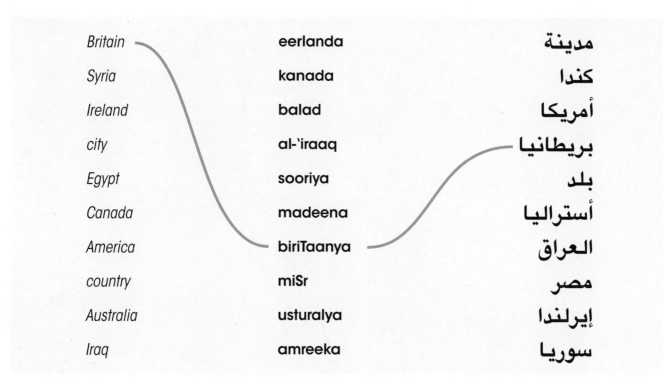

Britain	eerlanda	مدينة
Syria	kanada	كندا
Ireland	balad	أمريكا
city	al-ʿiraaq	بريطانيا
Egypt	sooriya	بلد
Canada	madeena	أستراليا
America	biriTaanya	العراق
country	miSr	مصر
Australia	usturalya	إيرلندا
Iraq	amreeka	سوريا

Where are the cities?

Now look at these cities and make sentences, using the word في fee (*in*), for example:
دمشق في سوريا. dimashq fee sooriya. *Damascus (is) in Syria.*

New York	Cairo	London	Damascus
نيو يورك	القاهرة	لندن	دمشق
nyoo yoork	al-qaahira	lundun	dimashq

Sydney	Washington	Toronto	Dublin
سيدني	واشنطن	تورنتو	دبلن
sidnee	waashinTun	torunto	dublin

Language Focus

It is straightforward to say where you're from. Use the phrase أنا من **ana min** (*I [am] from*) and add the name of the country or town:

> أنا من سوريا.   **ana min sooriya.** *I'm from Syria.*
>
> أنا من أمريكا.   **ana min amreeka.** *I'm from America.*
>
> أنا من القاهرة.   **ana min al-qaahira.** *I'm from Cairo.*

You could use في **fee** (*in*) or قريبة من **qareeba min** (*near to*) to be more specific:

> أنا من دمشق في سوريا.   **ana min dimashq fee sooriya.**
> *I'm from Damascus in Syria.*
>
> أنا من أكسفورد، مدينة قريبة من لندن.   **ana min oksfoord,**
> **madeena qareeba min lundun.** *I'm from Oxford, a city near London.*

If you want to ask someone where they are from, you need to use the question أنت من أين؟ **anta min ayna?** ("*you from where?*"). The pronunciation of "*you*" changes slightly if you are asking a female: **anti min ayna?** The basic spelling is the same, with the only difference being in the vowel markings (see page 90).

> أنت من أين يا يوسف؟   **anta min ayna yaa yoosef?**
> *Where are you from, Yoosef?*
>
> أنت من أين يا زينة؟   **anti min ayna yaa zayna?**
> *Where are you from, Zayna?*

8

Listen to these six people introducing themselves and see if you can understand where they are from: Yoosef, Lucy, Sameer, Harry, Fatima, Suzanne.

Where are they from?

Join the people to the places they are from, as in the example.
Listen again to track 8 on your CD if you need to remind yourself.

دمشق	لوسي
أكسفورد	فاطمة
تورنتو	سمير
برينستون	يوسف
بغداد	سوزان
القاهرة	هاري

Where are you from?

Now say where you're from.
Answer the questions on your audio CD.

9

 Key Words

10

أنا	ana	*I*	هي	hiya	*she*
أنت	anta/anti	*you*	من	min	*from*
هو	huwa	*he*	أين؟	ayna?	*where?*

 *Language Focus*

You now know how to ask and answer questions about where you're from:

أنت من أين؟   **anta/anti min ayna?** *Where are you from?*

أنا من إيرلندا.   **ana min eerlanda.** *I'm from Ireland.*

If you want to talk about where someone else is from, you can use هو **huwa** (*he*) or هي **hiya** (*she*):

هو من أين؟   **huwa min ayna?** *Where's he from?*

هو من أمريكا.   **huwa min amreeka.** *He's from America.*

هي من أين؟   **hiya min ayna?** *Where's she from?*

هي من دمشق في سوريا.   **hiya min dimashq fee sooriya.**
She's from Damascus in Syria.

You may have noticed that some countries and cities start with الـ **al-**, meaning *the*: العراق **al-'iraaq** (*Iraq*); القاهرة **al-qaahira** (*Cairo*).

You will learn more about **al-** in later topics. For the moment you need to know that when **al-** follows في **fee** (*in*), the combination is pronounced **fil**:

هو من بغداد في العراق.   **huwa min baghdaad fil-'iraaq.**
He's from Baghdad in Iraq.

Who's from where?

Make questions and answers about where these people are from.
Try to include a city that you know in the answer, as in the example.

2

هو من أين؟
huwa min ayna?
Where's he from?

هو من نيو يورك في أمريكا.
**huwa min nyoo yoork
fee amreeka.**
He's from New York in America.

1

4

3

6

5

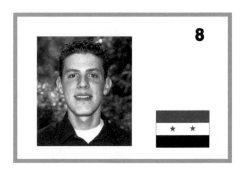

8

7

Listen and check

Listen to the conversation on your audio CD and decide if these sentences are true or false.

		True	False
1	The conversation takes place in the morning.	☐	☐
2	The woman's name is Sophie.	☐	☐
3	She comes from Canada.	☐	☐
4	The man's name is Munir.	☐	☐
5	He comes from Egypt.	☐	☐
6	They are already friends.	☐	☐

What does it mean?

Now read the Arabic you heard in the conversation and match it with English, as in the example.

I'm from Canada.	مساء الخير.
I'm from Egypt.	ما اسمك؟
My name's Louise.	أنا من مصر.
What's your name?	اسمي لويز.
Good evening.	أهلا.
Hello.	أنا من كندا.

What does it mean?

Read these sentences out loud and write the English next to each.

	اسمي زينة.	_My name's Louise._	اسمي لويز.
_____		_____	أنا من كندا.
_____	هو من أين؟		
_____	هو من لندن.	_____	منير من مصر.
_____	هي من أمريكا.	_____	ما اسمك؟

Now complete the description below, adding your own details. Read the description out loud.

في (country). (city/town) أنا من (name). اسمي ←

 # Key Words

12

	لبنان lubnaan	Lebanon	تونس toonis	Tunisia
	المغرب al-maghrib	Morocco	الجزائر al-jazaa'ir	Algeria
	الكويت al-kuwait	Kuwait	السعودية as-sa'oodiyya	Saudi

There are more than 20 Arabic-speaking countries spread throughout North Africa and Asia. Here are six more Arab nations with their flags. You'll need these to play the game.

The Flag Game

1. Tear out Game Card 2.

2. Find a die and counter(s).

3. Put the counter(s) on START.

4. Throw the die and move that number of squares.

5. When you land on a flag, you must ask and answer the appropriate question for that country. For example:

أنت من أين؟ anta/anti min ayna?
(*Where are you from?*)

أنا من بريطانيا. ana min biriTaanya.
(*I'm from Britain.*)

6. If you can't remember the question or answer, you must go back to the square you came from. You must throw the exact number to finish.

7. You can challenge yourself or play with a friend.

 ## Key Words

كرسي	kursee	*chair*	باب	baab	*door*
مائدة	maa'ida	*table*	شباك	shubbaak	*window*
تليفزيون	tileefizyoon	*television*	قلم	qalam	*pen*
كتاب	kitaab	*book*	مجلة	majalla	*magazine*
حقيبة	Haqeeba	*bag*	كنبة	kanaba	*sofa*
كمبيوتر	kumbiyootir	*computer*	تليفون	tileefoon	*telephone*

13

Listen first to the key words on your CD. Then look around the room you're in and try to use the words to name as many objects as you can find. Count how many Arabic words you use.

Then look back at the list and review the words you couldn't remember. Try again to name objects and see if you can beat your first score.

24

What does it mean?

Match the Arabic with the pictures, then write the pronunciation and the English, as in the example.

قلم _____

كنبة _____

حقيبة _____

كمبيوتر _____

شباك *shubbaak (window)*

باب _____

مائدة _____

كرسي _____

تليفزيون _____

مجلة _____

تليفون _____

كتاب _____

Word Square

Can you find the 8 key words in the word square?
Circle them and write the English, as in the example.

ج	بـ	شـ	ة	بـ	يـ	ق	حـ
ب	ا	ت	كـ	جـ	و	غـ	لـ
م	ـة	بـ	نـ	كـ	ع	ز	ظ
ي	جـ	يـ	م	لـ	ق	ا	ذ
ع	تـ	جـ	لـ	سـ	م	ا	تـ
ث	ز	بـ	كـ	ا	بـ	شـ	ضـ
ن	و	فـ	يـ	لـ	تـ	م	و
ي	سـ	ر	كـ	نـ	بـ	ا	بـ

bag

_____

_____

_____

_____

_____

Odd One Out

Which is the odd one out? Circle the word that doesn't belong in each row.

سمير * سوزان * تليفزيون * فاطمة

مائدة * كرسي * باب * اسم

مجلة * كتاب * قلم * مساء

مصر * تليفون * أمريكا * العراق

صباح الخير * كنبة * أهلا * مع السلامة

Language Focus

Arabic nouns (naming words) are either *masculine* (هو **huwa** *he*) or *feminine* (هي **hiya** *she*). There is no equivalent of the English *it*. Nearly all feminine nouns either end in a special feminine ending **-a** (ة) known as **taa marbooTa**, or are words which refer to female people (or both). You can assume a word is masculine unless it falls into one of these two categories.

masculine nouns	*feminine nouns*
يوسف (**yoosef** *Yoosef*)	زينة (**zayna** *Zayna*)
اسم (**ism** *name*)	مجلة (**majalla** *magazine*)
كتاب (**kitaab** *book*)	مائدة (**maa'ida** *table*)
ولد (**walad** *boy*)	بنت (**bint** *girl*)

This in Arabic is هذا **haaтнa** for masculine nouns and هذه **haaтнihi** for feminine nouns. There is no equivalent of the English *a/an* or *is*, so you can make simple sentences using *this* + noun:

> هذا كتاب. **haaтнa kitaab.**   *This (is a) book.*
>
> هذه مجلة. **haaтнihi majalla.**   *This (is a) magazine.*

Use ما **maa** (*what?*) and هل **hal** (a general question marker) to make questions. *No* is لا **laa** and *yes* is نعم **na'am**.

> ما هذا؟ هذا قلم. **maa haaтнa? haaтнa qalam.**
> *What's this? It's a pen.*
>
> هل هذه مجلة؟ **hal haaтнihi majalla?**   *Is this a magazine?*
>
> نعم، هي مجلة./لا، هو كتاب. **na'am, hiya majalla./laa, huwa kitaab.** *Yes, it's a magazine./No, it's a book*

 Ask and answer the questions.
Follow the prompts on your CD.

14

What's this?

Look at the photos of everyday objects from unusual angles. Then read the sentences and decide which picture they describe, as in the example.

5 هذا باب. ـــــــ	1 هذا كرسي. _e_
6 هذا تليفزيون. ـــــــ	2 هذا كمبيوتر. ـــــــ
7 هذا قلم. ـــــــ	3 هذه كنبة. ـــــــ
8 هذه حقيبة. ـــــــ	4 هذا تليفون. ـــــــ

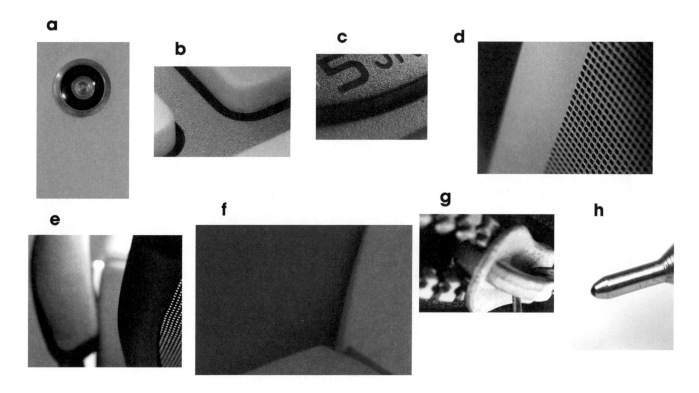

a
b
c
d
e
f
g
h

Key Words

15

شاي	shaay	*tea*	كعكة	ka'ka	*cake*	
قهوة	qahwa	*coffee*	فلافل	falaafil	*falafel*	
سندويتش	sandawitsh	*sandwich*	فطيرة	faTeera	*pancake*	

Language Focus

The easiest way to ask for something in a café or store is to use the phrase ممكن ...؟ **mumkin ...?** (approximately meaning *possible ...?*), or the more formal phrase أريد ... **ureed ...** (*I'd like ...*), and add *please*: من فضلك **min faDlak** (**min faDlik** when talking to a woman).

Use و **wa** (*and*) to ask for more than one thing. Notice that و **wa** is written next to the following word without a space in Arabic script:

ممكن شاي من فضلك؟   **mumkin shaay min faDlak?**
May I have a tea, please?

أريد قهوة وفطيرة من فضلك.   **ureed qahwa wa-faTeera min faDlak.**
I'd like a coffee and a pancake, please.

Here you are is تفضل **tafaDDal** to a man or تفضلي **tafaDDalee** to a woman.

ممكن سندويتش من فضلك؟   **mumkin sandawitsh min faDlak?**
May I have a sandwich, please?

تفضلي يا مدام.   **tafaDDalee yaa madaam.**
Here you are, madam.

Who orders what?

What are the customers ordering? Listen to your CD
and tick what they order, as in the example.

16

	tea	coffee	sandwich	cake	falafel	pancake
Customer 1		✓			✓	
Customer 2						
Customer 3						
Customer 4						
Customer 5						

Now look at the table and pretend you are ordering for yourself. Try to use the
two ways you know of asking for something:

mumkin qahwa wa-falaafil min faDlak? ممكن قهوة وفلافل من فضلك؟

ureed qahwa wa-falaafil min faDlak. أريد قهوة وفلافل من فضلك.

Unscramble the conversation

Can you put this conversation in the correct order?

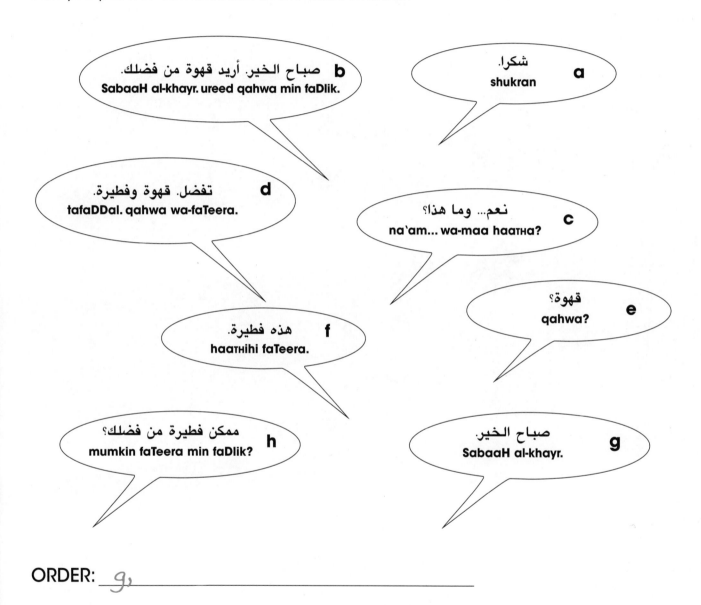

b صباح الخير. أريد قهوة من فضلك.
SabaaH al-khayr. ureed qahwa min faDlik.

a شكرا.
shukran

d تفضل. قهوة وفطيرة.
tafaDDal. qahwa wa-faTeera.

c نعم... وما هذا؟
na'am... wa-maa haaтна?

f هذه فطيرة.
haaтнihi faTeera.

e قهوة؟
qahwa?

h ممكن فطيرة من فضلك؟
mumkin faTeera min faDlik?

g صباح الخير.
SabaaH al-khayr.

ORDER: _g,_____

Now check your answer with the
conversation on your audio CD.

17

At the café

Your turn to order now. Look at the menu below and then you'll be ready to order from the waiter on your CD.

18

قهوة علي بابا

شاي

قهوة

كولا

سندويتش

كعكة

طاجن

فطيرة

فلافل

Did you work out what the café is called? Yes, it's Ali Baba (علي بابا) !

The Café Game

1. Cut out the picture cards from Game Card 3.

2. Put the cards into a bag.

3. Shake the bag.

4. Pull out a card without looking.

5. Ask for the item on the card. For example:

ممكن شاي من فضلك؟

mumkin shaay min faDlak?

(*Can I have [a] tea, please?*)

6. If you can ask the question out loud quickly and fluently, then put the card aside. If not, then put it back into the bag.

7. See how long it takes you to get all of the cards out of the bag. Or play with a friend and see who can collect the most cards.

GAME CARD 3 (see page 33)

Picture cards:

Key Words

19

غرفة	ghurfa	*room*	بيت	bayt	*house*
ثلاجة	thallaaja	*refrigerator*	شجر	shajar	*trees*
ستار	sitaar	*curtains*	سيارة	sayyaara	*car*
فرن	furn	*stove*	قطة	qiTTa	*cat*
سرير	sareer	*bed*	كلب	kalb	*dog*
صورة	Soora	*picture*	فأر	faar	*mouse*

 ## Language Focus

Although Arabic does not have an equivalent of *a/an*, it does have an equivalent of the: ‏الـ‎ *al-*. The word ‏الـ‎ *al-* is written joined to the noun it refers to:

كلب	kalb *(a) dog*		الكلب	al-kalb *the dog*
غرفة	ghurfa *(a) room*		الغرفة	al-ghurfa *the room*

With approximately half the letters of the Arabic alphabet the "l" sound of **al** is assimilated ("taken over") by the sound of the first letter of the following word. These letters are called *sun letters*. Try to recognize this assimilation but don't worry too much as you will be understood if you pronounce the "l".

سيارة	sayyaara *(a) car*		السيارة	as-sayyaara *the car*
صورة	Soora *(a) picture*		الصورة	aS-Soora *the picture*

What does it mean?

Join the Arabic to the pronunciation and write down what the words mean in English.

_____	sareer	فرن
_____	bayt	كلب
_____	kalb	غرفة
_____	sitaar	قطة
stove	furn	سرير
_____	ghurfa	صورة
_____	Soora	ثلاجة
_____	shajar	شجر
_____	sayyaara	بيت
_____	qiTTa	سيارة
_____	thallaaja	فأر
_____	faar	ستار

What can you see?

Look at the picture and tick (✔) the things you can see, as in the example.

☐ كلب	✔ قطة
☐ ستار	☐ شباك
☐ شجر	☐ فرن
☐ سرير	☐ باب
☐ صورة	☐ حقيبة
☐ ثلاجة	☐ تليفزيون
☐ كتاب	☐ كمبيوتر
☐ سيارة	☐ قلم
☐ تليفون	☐ مجلة
☐ مائدة	☐ كرسي

🔑 Key Words

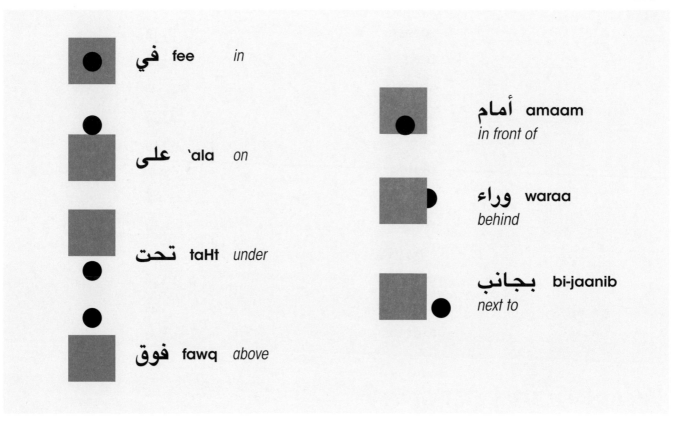

في **fee** *in*

على **'ala** *on*

تحت **taHt** *under*

فوق **fawq** *above*

أمام **amaam** *in front of*

وراء **waraa** *behind*

بجانب **bi-jaanib** *next to*

🔍 Language Focus

When...الـ **al-** (*the*) is preceded by a word which ends with a vowel, the **a** of **al-** is dropped. The spelling is not affected.

الغرفة **al-ghurfa** *the room* → في الغرفة **fil-ghurfa** *in the room*

الكرسي **al-kursee** *the chair* → على الكرسي **ala l-kursee** *on the chair*

Practise saying where things are on your CD.

21

Which word?

Put a circle around the word that correctly describes each picture, as in the example.

1 السيارة (أمام) البيت.
في

2 السرير فوق الشباك.
تحت

3 الصورة أمام الكنبة.
فوق

4 الكمبيوتر على المائدة.
بجانب

5 الثلاجة فوق الفرن.
بجانب

6 القطة تحت الكرسي.
على

7 البنت وراء الباب.
تحت

8 الكلب أمام السيارة.
في

 *Language Focus*

A useful Arabic phrase when describing places is هناك (**hunaaka**), which is the equivalent of the English *there is* or *there are*.

Arabic doesn't use *is* or *are*, so this phrase doesn't change depending on whether you are talking about one thing (*singular*) or more than one thing (*plural*). You simply use هناك (**hunaaka**) followed by the noun:

> هناك بنك. **hunaaka bank.** *There is a bank.*
>
> هناك شجر. **hunaaka shajar.** *There are trees.*

In this way you can make simple descriptions using the positional words and vocabulary you have already met in this book:

> هناك بنك في المدينة. **hunaaka bank fil-madeena.**
> *There is a bank in the town.*
>
> هناك شجر بجانب البيت. **hunaaka shajar bi-jaanib il-bayt.**
> *There are trees next to the house.*

If you want to ask a question, simply add the question marker هل (**hal**) at the beginning:

> هل هناك بنك في المدينة؟ **hal hunaaka bank fil-madeena?**
> *Is there a bank in the town?*
>
> هل هناك شجر؟ **hal hunaaka shajar?**
> *Are there [any] trees?*

> Look around the room you are in at the moment, or think of a room you know well. Can you describe where some of the things are using هناك?

Where are the mice?

See how many mice you can find in the picture and make sentences about them using the sentence table, as in the example.

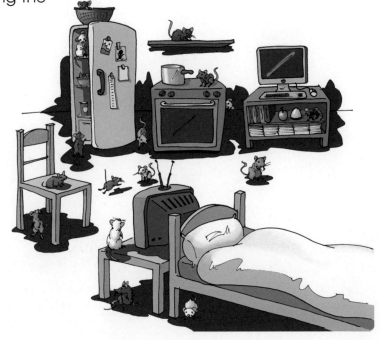

Example:

هناك فأر تحت السرير.

There's a mouse under the bed.

الفرن.	في ...	
الكمبيوتر.	على ...	
التليفزيون.	فوق ...	
الكرسي.	تحت ...	هناك فأر ...
الكنبة.		
السرير.	بجانب ...	
المائدة.	أمام ...	
الثلاجة.	وراء ...	

Language Focus

The most common regular Arabic plural is the ending ات -**aat**. The words below from topics 3 and 4 can be made plural using ات -**aat**. Notice that if the singular ends with the feminine -**a** (ة), you must remove this before adding ات -**aat**.

	singular	*plural*
television	تليفزيون tileefizyoon	تليفزيونات tileefizyoonaat
computer	كمبيوتر kumbiyoortir	كمبيوترات kumbiyootiraat
magazine	مجلة majalla	مجلات majallaat
telephone	تليفون tileefoon	تليفونات tileefoonaat
refrigerator	ثلاجة thallaaja	ثلاجات thallaajaat
car	سيارة sayyaara	سيارات sayyaaraat

However, many Arabic plurals are irregular, similar to the English *man/men* or *mouse/ mice*. As a beginner, you'll need to learn these plurals individually. Later, patterns will emerge that will help you. From now on we will add useful plurals in brackets in the Key Words panels. Here are the other words you already know with their plurals:

	singular	*plural*
chair	كرسي kursee	كراسي karaasee
table	مائدة maa-ida	موائد mawaa-id
book	كتاب kitaab	كتب kutub
bag	حقيبة Haqeeba	حقائب Haqaa-ib
door	باب baab	أبواب abwaab
window	شباك shubbaak	شبابيك shabaabeek
pen	قلم qalam	أقلام aqlaam
room	غرفة ghurfa	غرف ghuraf
curtains	ستار sitaar	ستائر sataa'ir
stove	فرن furn	أفران afraan
bed	سرير sareer	أسرة asirra
picture	صورة Soora	صور Suwar
house	بيت bayt	بيوت buyoot
tree	شجرة shajara	شجر shajar
dog	كلب kalb	كلاب kilaab
cat	قطة qiTTa	قطط qiTaT
mouse	فأر faar	فئران fi'raan

The opposite of هناك **hunaaka** (*there is/are*) is ليس هناك
laysa hunaaka (*there isn't/aren't*):

هناك سيارات أمام البيت. **hunaaka sayyaaraat amaam il-bayt.**
There are cars in front of the house.

ليس هناك سيارات أمام البيت. **laysa hunaaka sayyaaraat amaam il-bayt.**
There aren't any cars in front of the house.

Listen and learn

You'll find an activity on your CD to help you remember the plurals.

22

True or False?

Decide if the sentences describing
the picture are true or false.

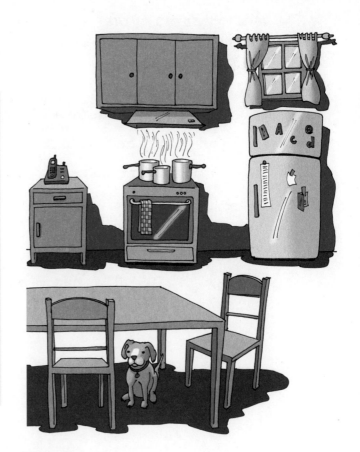

		True	False
هناك ثلاجة في الغرفة.	1	☑	☐
هناك كلب تحت المائدة.	2	☐	☐
الفرن بجانب الثلاجة.	3	☐	☐
هناك شجر وراء الثلاجة.	4	☐	☐
ليس هناك فأر تحت المائدة.	5	☐	☐
هناك شباك في الغرفة.	6	☐	☐
ليس هناك ستائر على الشباك.	7	☐	☐
التليفون على الفرن.	8	☐	☐
هناك سرير في الغرفة.	9	☐	☐
ليس هناك تليفزيون في الغرفة.	10	☐	☐

Language Review

You're half way through this programme – congratulations! This is a good time to summarize the main language points covered so far in *Read & Speak Arabic*.

1 Arabic has two genders: *masculine* and *feminine*. Nearly all feminine words either end in ة **-a** (e.g. غرفة **ghurfa** *room*) or refer to female people (e.g. بنت **bint** *girl*).

2 الـ **al-** means *the*. There is no equivalent of *a/an*. Certain letters of the alphabet assimilate the "l" sound of **al-**. The "a" of **al-** is dropped when preceded by a vowel. These changes affect only the pronunciation, not the spelling.

قلم **qalam** *(a) pen*	القلم **al-qalam** *the pen*
صور **Suwar** *pictures*	الصور **aS-Suwar** *the pictures*
حقيبة **Haqeeba** *(a) bag*	في الحقيبة **fil-Haqeeba** *in the bag*

3 You can ask for something by using the phrase ...ممكن **mumkin...** or ...أريد **ureed...**, but من فضلك **min faDlak** is fairly essential either way.

4 The verb *to be* (*am/is/are*) is not generally used in the present. Simple sentences and questions can be formed without the verb *to be*:

اسمي سمير. **ismee sameer.** *My name (is) Sameer.*

أنا من العراق. **ana min al-'iraaq.** *I (am) from Iraq.*

هذا قلم. **haaтна qalam.** *This (is a) pen.*

هو من أين؟ **huwa min ayna?** *Where (is) he from?*

هل القلم تحت السرير؟ **hal al-qalam taHt as-sareer?**
(Is) the pen under the bed?

هناك كلاب في البيت. **hunaaka kilaab fil-bayt.**
There (are) dogs in the house.

5 The most common *regular* plural ending is ات **-aat**. Many Arabic plurals are *irregular* and have to be learnt individually.

My Room

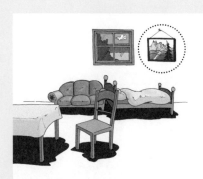

1. Tear out Game Card 4 at the back of your book and cut out the small pictures of items around the house (leave the sentence-build cards at the bottom of the sheet for the moment).

2. Stick the pictures wherever you like on the scene below.

3. Cut out the sentence-build cards from Game Card 4. Make as many sentences as you can describing your room. For example:

.	السرير	فوق	صورة	هناك

hunaaka Soora fawq as-sareer.

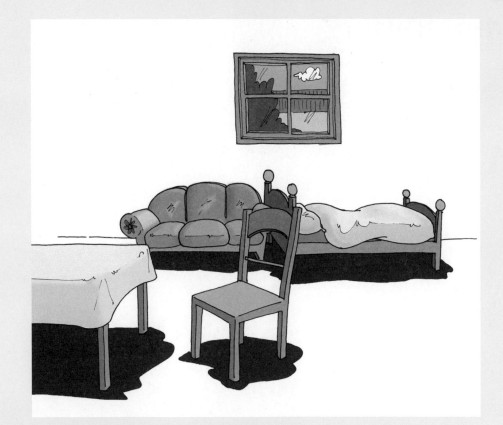

 Key Words

كبير	kabeer	big	طويل	Taweel	tall/long
صغير	Sagheer	small	قصير	qaSeer	short
قديم	qadeem	old	غالٍ	ghaalee	expensive
جديد	jadeed	new	رخيص	rakheeS	inexpensive
جدا	jiddan	very			

Can you remember?

Cover the Key Words panel on this page. Then see if you can write out the pronunciation and meaning of the words below, as in the example.

رخيص r_a_k_h_e_e_S _inexpensive_   قصير q _ _ _ _ r _____

طويل T _ _ _ _ l _____   غالٍ g _ _ _ _ _ e _____

صغير S _ _ _ _ _ r _____   كبير k _ _ _ _ r _____

قديم q _ _ _ _ m _____   جديد j _ _ _ _ d _____

جدا j _ _ _ _ n _____

 # Language Focus

Descriptive words, or *adjectives*, come <u>after</u> the word they are describing. If the noun being described is feminine, the adjective will also have the feminine ة -a ending:

بيت كبير **bayt kabeer** *(a) big house (masc.)*

سيارة جديدة **sayyaara jadeeda** *(a) new car (fem.)*

If you want to say <u>*the* big house</u>, etc., then both the noun and the adjective need to start with ال **al-**:

البيت الكبير **al-bayt al-kabeer** *the big house*

السيارة الجديدة **as-sayyaara al-jadeeda** *the new car*

Note that when only the noun has ال **al-** then the meaning changes. By putting a definite noun (with ال **al-**) followed by an indefinite adjective (without ال **al-**), a sentence is created meaning *The house is big*, etc:

البيت كبير. **al-bayt kabeer.** *The house is big.*

الكنبة جديدة. **al-kanaba jadeeda.** *The sofa is new.*

الشاي رخيص. **ash-shaay rakheeS.** *The tea is inexpensive.*

جدا **jiddan** (*very*) comes after the adjective:

كرسي صغير جدا **kursee Sagheer jiddan** *(a) very small chair*

الكتاب قديم جدا. **al-kitaab qadeem jiddan.** *The book is very old.*

Note the unusual ending of غال (*expensive*), formally pronounced **ghaalin**, but more commonly pronounced **ghaalee**. The feminine is غالية (**ghaalya**).

قلم غالٍ **qalam ghaalee** *(an) expensive pen*

سيارة غالية **sayyaara ghaalya** *(an) expensive car*

What does it mean?

Match the Arabic with the pictures. Then read the Arabic out loud
and write the English next to each, as in the example.

قهوة صغيرة _____

صورة غالية _____

كلب صغير *(a) small dog* _____

كنبة جديدة _____

بيت صغير _____

سيارة قديمة جدا _____

سندويتش كبير _____

شجر طويل جدا _____

24

Listen and check

Listen to the conversation at the car rental company and decide if these sentences are true or false.

		True	False
1	The conversation takes place in the evening.	☐	☐
2	The woman wants to rent a car.	☐	☐
3	She thinks the Mercedes is very expensive.	☐	☐
4	She thinks the Fiat is too big.	☐	☐
5	She likes the Peugeot.	☐	☐
6	Her name is Amira Zidan.	☐	☐
7	She's from Amman in Jordan.	☐	☐

Unscramble the sentences

Look at the scrambled sentences below and write the correct order.

Example:

a	b	d	c
صباح	الخير	سيارة	أريد

3

☐	☐	☐	☐
كبيرة	أريد	جدا	سيارة

1

☐	☐	☐
سامي	اسمي	أميرة

4

☐	☐	☐	☐
هذه	السيارة	غالية	جدا

2

☐	☐	☐
تونس	أنا	من

Language Focus

You already know the Arabic pronouns **ana/anta** (**anti**)/**huwa/hiya** (*I*/*you*/*he*/*she*) and the possessive endings **-ee/-ak(-ik)** (*my*/*your*). Now here are the other pronouns and possessive endings:

	pronoun	*possessive ending*
I	أنا **ana**	ـي **-ee:** اسمي **ismee** *my name*
you (masc.)	أنت **anta**	ـك **-ak:** قلمك **qalamak** *your (masc.) pen*
you (fem.)	أنت **anti**	ـك **-ik:** بلدك **baladik** *your (fem.) country*
he	هو **huwa**	ـه **-uh:** كتابه **kitaabuh** *his book*
she	هي **hiya**	ـها **-haa:** سريرها **sareerhaa** *her bed*
we	نحن **naHnu**	ـنا **-naa:** بيتنا **baytnaa** *our house*
you (pl.)	أنتم **antum**	ـكم **-kum:** غرفكم **ghurafkum** *your (pl.) rooms*
they	هم **hum**	ـهم **-hum:** بيوتهم **buyoothum** *their houses*

Notice that there are three ways of saying *you* and *your* depending on whether you are talking to a male (أنت **anta**), a female (أنت **anti**) or a group (أنتم **antum**).

You can combine the possessive endings with the word عند **'inda** (*with/at*) to express the meaning of "having" something:

عندنا سيارة جديدة. **'indanaa sayyaara jadeeda.**
We have a new car.

سمير عنده بيت في لندن. **sameer 'induh bayt fee lundun.**
Sameer has a house in London.

The final a is removed from عند **'inda** when ـي **-ee**, ـك **-ak/-ik**, or ـه **-uh** are added:

عندي كلب كبير. **'indee kalb kabeer.** *I have a big dog.*

هل عندك قلم؟ **hal 'indak qalam?** *Do you have a pen?*

 Now you can take part in a conversation with the car rental company. Follow the prompts on your audio CD.

25

 Key Words

26

جميل	jameel	*beautiful*		شعر	sha'r	*hair*
قبيح	qabeeH	*ugly*		رأس	ra's	*head*
سمين	sameen	*fat*		أنف	anf	*nose*
رفيع	rafee`	*thin*		فم	fam	*mouth*
غريب	ghareeb	*strange*		ذيل	THayl	*tail*

By now you're probably feeling much more confident about reading and speaking Arabic. Maybe you'd like to try writing the script for yourself. If so, make sure you get hold of a guide to handwriting the Arabic script or ask a native speaker to show you. It's not always obvious how to form the letters or how to join them by looking at the printed script.

Which word?

Circle the correct word to match the translation, as in the example.

1 فأر   باب   (رأس)   فم   *head*

2 رخيص   غريب   غالٍ   غرفة   *strange*

3 سرير   سيارة   صغير   سمين   *fat*

4 باب   فأر   فم   قلم   *mouth*

5 ذيل   صورة   باب   بيت   *tail*

6 صغير   شعر   شجرة   شباك   *hair*

7 جديد   جدا   جميل   قبيح   *beautiful*

8 أنف   فرن   فم   أقلام   *nose*

9 رخيص   رفيع   سرير   غريب   *thin*

10 قصير   قلم   قديم   قبيح   *ugly*

At the pet show

Can you use the words in the box to complete the description of these pets?

3 هذا	**2** جدا	**1** أنفها
6 القطة	**5** قصير	**4** طويل

هذه ___6___ جميلة. ذيلها ___ جدا و ___ صغير وجميل.

___ الكلب قبيح وغريب. ذيله ___ وانفه كبير ___!

What does it look like?

What does the creature look like? Make as many sentences as you can describing what it looks like.

We've included a checklist of features you could describe and adjectives you could use.

Example:

هو سمين وفمه صغير.

huwa sameen wa-famuh Sagheer.

He's fat and his mouth is small.

جميل	beautiful
قبيح	ugly
سمين	fat
رفيع	thin
كبير	big
صغير	small
طويل	tall/long
قصير	short
غريب	strange
جدا	very

شعر	hair
رأس	head
أنف	nose
فم	mouth
ذيل	tail

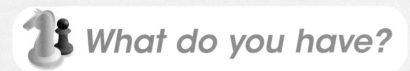

What do you have?

1. Cut out the picture cards from Game Card 5 and put them in a bag.

2. Cut out set 2 adjective cards and put them in a different bag.

3. Pull out one card from each bag without looking.

4. Make a sentence to match the cards you have chosen, for example:

   عندي كمبيوتر قديم.

   'indee kumbiyootir qadeem.

   (I have an old computer.)

   Don't forget to make the adjective feminine if the noun is feminine:

   عندي سيارة جديدة.

   'indee sayyaara jadeeda.

   (I have a new car.)

5. Keep playing until all the cards have been chosen.

6. You can put the cards back in the bag and start again – each time the sentences will be different.

GAME CARD 5 (see page 53)

Picture cards:

Adjective cards:

جديد	طويل	قبيح	غريب
قديم	صغير	قصير	سمين
جميل	كبير	غالٍ	رخيص

قديم

Key Words

27

مطار maTaar	airport	
(pl. -aat)		
مدرسة madrasa	school	
(pl. madaaris)		
فندق funduq	hotel	
(pl. fanaadiq)		
بنك bank	bank	
(pl. bunook)		
مطعم maT'am	restaurant	
(pl. maTaa'im)		
محطّة maHaTTa	station	
(pl. -aat)		

حديقة Hadeeqa	park
(pl. Hadaa'iq)	
جسر jisr	bridge
(pl. jusoor)	
شارع shaari'	street
(pl. shawaari')	
شارع الملك	Malik (King) Street
shaari' al-malik	
متحف matHaf	museum
(pl. mataaHif)	
أين...؟ ayna...?	where's...?

28

You are new in town and are asking an Arabic-speaking friend about the facilities. Follow the prompts on your audio CD.

Language Focus

Modern Arabic has many loan words imported from other languages, particularly English. You have already met some, such as كمبيوتر **kumbiyootir**, تليفون **tilifoon**, بنك **bank**, and سندويتش **sandawitsh**. Other examples of words you will recognize easily are راديو **raadyo** (*radio*), فيديو **feedyo** (*video*), كولا **kola** (*cola*), and تاكسي **taaksee** (*taxi*).

In an attempt to minimize foreign influence on the language, "purer" Arabic alternatives have developed for most of these words, for example, مصرف **maSraf** for bank (literally "place for changing [money]"), آلة حاسبة **aala Haasiba** ("calculating instrument") for computer, and سيارة أجرة **sayyaarat ujra** ("car for rent") for taxi. These alternatives are sometimes used in more formal language.

Questions and answers

Match the questions with their answers, as in the example.

الفندق أمام الجسر.	أين الجسر؟
هي قريبة من هنا.	أين فندق الأميرة؟
الجسر بجانب المحطة.	هل هناك مطعم في الفندق؟
البنك في شارع الملك.	أين المدرسة؟
نعم، مطعم كبير.	أين البنك؟

 ## Key Words

تاكسي taksee	taxi	طائرة Taa'ira	aeroplane
(pl. -yaat)		(pl. -aat)	
أتوبيس otobees	bus	مركب markib	boat
(pl. -aat)		(pl. maraakib)	
قطار qiTaar	train	دراجة darraaja	bicycle
(pl. -aat)		(pl. -aat)	

 ## Language Focus

To express how you travel, use بـ bi- (*by/ with*) + means of transportation.
بـ bi- is written joined to the following word.

When talking in general, Arabic tends to use the definite الـ al-. When combined with بـ bi- the combination becomes بالـ bil- with the "l" assimilating if the following word starts with a sun letter (see page 34):

بالقطار bil-qiTaar *by train*	بالأتوبيس bil-otobees *by bus*
بالتاكسي bit-taksee *by taxi*	بالدراجة bid-darraaja *by bicycle*
بالمركب bil-markib *by boat*	بالطائرة biT-Taa'ira *by aeroplane*

Word Square

Can you find the 7 different means of transportation in the word square?
Write out the meaning for the words you have found.

س	بـ	شـ	ة	ر	ا	يـ	سـ
ر	ـا	ط	ق	جـ	و	ئـ	لـ
س	يـ	بـ	و	ت	أ	ز	ظـ
ي	جـ	يـ	مـ	بـ	ك	ر	مـ
ع	تـ	ج	لـ	سـ	مـ	أ	ت
ـة	جـ	ا	ر	د	بـ	شـ	ضـ
ة	ر	ئـ	ـا	ط	و	ت	أ
ع	مـ	ي	سـ	ك	ا	ت	شـ

car _____

_____

_____

_____

_____

_____

 Language Focus

The **hamza** (ء), which appears on or under **alif** at the beginning of a word, can also be found in the middle of words, usually written on a **sinna** ("tooth"): ئـ. You pronounce the **hamza** as a pause between the two syllables.

Words you have met which include this spelling feature are:

طائرة **Taa'ira** *aeroplane*   حدائق **Hadaa'iq** *parks*

مائدة **maa'ida** *table*   حقائب **Haqaa'ib** *bags*

موائد **mawaa'id** *tables*   الجزائر **al-jazaa'ir** *Algeria*

🔑 Key Words

30

لو سمحت!	excuse me!	على اليمين	on the right	
law samaHt (*fem:* law samaHti)		`ala l-yameen		
... من أين؟	How do I get to ...?	على اليسار	on the left	
... min ayna?		`ala l-yasaar		
يمين yameen	right	على طول	(go) straight ahead	
يسار yasaar	left	`ala Tool		
أول شارع	the first street	هنا huna	here	
awwal shaari`		ثم thumma	then	
ثاني شارع	the second street	بعد ذلك	after that	
thaanee shaari`		ba`da THaalik		

Ask for directions to places around town. Follow the prompts on your audio CD.

31

Language Focus

As well as asking the question ؟من أين ... ... **min ayna?** (literally *... from where?*), you'll need to understand basic directions. In addition to the phrases in the Key Words panel, you might also hear the instruction ... خذ **khutн ...** (*take ...*) used to give directions:

خذ تاكسي من هنا.   **khutн taaksee min huna.**
Take a taxi from here.

خذ أول شارع على اليمين.   **khutн awwal shaari' 'ala l-yameen.**
Take the first street on the right.

When talking to a female, add **-ee** to the end of the instruction – خذي **khutнee**:

خذي ثاني شارع على اليسار.   **khutнee thaanee shaari' 'ala l-yasaar.** *Take the second street on the left.*

At, as in *at the bridge*, is عند **'inda** which you already know from expressing possession:

خذ الأتوبيس عند الجسر.   **khutн al-otoobees 'inda l-jisr.**
Take the bus at the bridge.

خذي أول شارع على اليسار عند المستشفى.
khutнee awwal shaari' 'ala l-yasaar 'inda l-mustashfa.
Take (fem.) the first street on the left at the hospital.

Which way?

Make questions and answers, as in the example.

لو سمحت، المحطة من أين؟

law samaHt, al-maHaTTa min ayna?

Excuse me, how do I get to the station?

خذ أول شارع على اليسار.

khuTH awwal shaari'' 'ala l-yasaar

Take the first street on the left.

 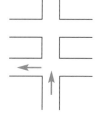

2

 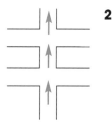

1

 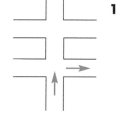

4

3

6

 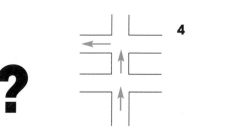  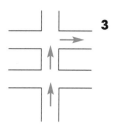

5

Around town

Below is a plan of a small town with some landmarks shown.
Starting from **You are here** try to give directions to the following places:

المستشفى	فندق كريم	الحديقة	محطة الأتوبيس
the hospital	*Karim Hotel*	*the park*	*the bus station*

For example, your directions to the hospital could be something like this:

على طول من هنا وبعد ذلك خذ أول شارع على اليمين عند البنك.

المستشفى قريبة من الجسر.

'ala Tool min huna wa-ba'da THaalik kHuTH awwal shaari' 'ala l-yameen 'inda l-bank.

al-mustashfa qareeba min al-jisr.

Go straight ahead from here and after that take the first street on the right at the bank.

The hospital is near the bridge.

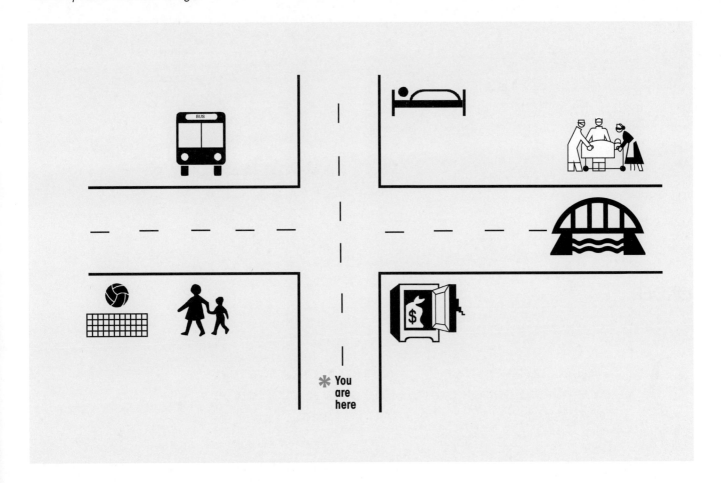

Unscramble the conversation

Can you put this conversation in the correct order?

a شارع الملك؟ خذي الأتوبيس.

b نعم؟

d خذي يسار من هنا ويمين عند الحديقة. محطة الأتوبيس بجانب البنك.

c شارع الملك من أين؟

e لو سمحت!

f شكرا.

g أين محطة الأتوبيس؟

ORDER: _e,_____

Did you also work out whether the person asking is male or female?	Check your answer with the conversation on your audio CD.

32

Town Planning

33

1. Cut out the pictures of places around town from Game Card 6.

2. Listen to the first set of directions for the bank on your audio CD.

3. Pause the CD and stick the picture of the bank in the correct place on the town map on your game card.

4. Listen to the next set of directions and stick down the appropriate picture.

5. Repeat for all the directions until you have all your pictures stuck down on the map.

6. Looking at the completed map, you could try to give directions to the various places yourself. For example:

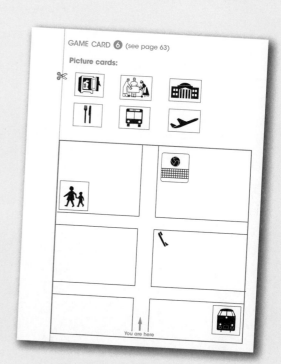

خذ ثاني شارع على اليسار.
البنك على اليمين بجانب المدرسة.

книтн thaanee shaari' 'ala l-yasaar.
al-bank 'ala l-yameen bi-jaanib al-madrasa.
(Take the second street on the left. The bank is on the right next to the school.)

 *Key Words*

34

زوجة	zawja	wife		أخ	akh	brother
					(*pl.* ikhwa)	
زوج	zawj	husband				
				طفل	Tifl	child
أم	umm	mother			(*pl.* aTfaal)	
				ابنة	ibna	daughter
أب	ab	father			(*pl.* banaat)	
				ابن	ibn	son
أخت	ukht	sister			(*pl.* abnaa')	
(*pl.* akhawaat)						

Find a photograph album and point to your relatives and friends, saying who they are in Arabic.

For example:

هذا أخي. haатна akhee. (*This is my brother.*);

هذه سارة وزوجها سامي. haатнihi saara wa-zawjhaa saamee.
(*This is Sarah and her husband Sammy.*)

Look back at page 48 if you want to review the possessive endings.

 ## Language Focus

You can use عند **'inda** to talk about your family:

> عندي أخ اسمه مارك. **'indee akh ismuh maark.**
> *I have a brother whose name is Mark. (lit: "... his name is Mark")*
>
> هل عندك أطفال؟ **hal 'indak aTfaal?**
> *Do you have children?*

The opposite is ليس عند **laysa 'inda:**

> سميرة ليس عندها أخ. **sameera laysa 'indahaa akh.**
> *Sameera doesn't have a brother.*
>
> ليس عندنا بنات. **laysa 'indanaa banaat.**
> *We don't have any daughters.*

What does it mean?

Join the Arabic to the pronunciation and the English, as in the example.

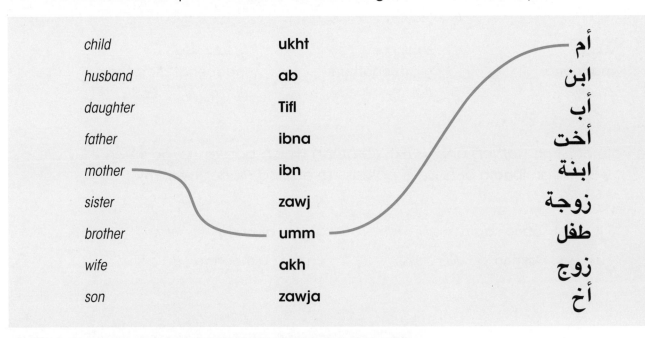

child	ukht	أم
husband	ab	ابن
daughter	Tifl	أب
father	ibna	أخت
mother	ibn	ابنة
sister	zawj	زوجة
brother	umm	طفل
wife	akh	زوج
son	zawja	أخ

Language Focus

You know how to use possessive endings: بنتي **bintee** *my daughter*; زوجك **zawjik** *your husband*, etc.

To express possession using a noun (the equivalent of the English *'s* or *of* as in *Ahmed's son* or *the door of the school*), Arabic puts the two words directly together in the order *possessed + possessor*. This possessive construction is called إضافة **iDaafa** (*addition*). The *first* noun in an **iDaafa** doesn't have the article الـ **al**, even if the meaning is definite:

ابن أحمد   **ibn aHmad**   *son + Ahmed = Ahmed's son*

باب المدرسة   **baab al-madrasa**   *door + the school = [the] door of the school*

أنف الكلب   **anf al-kalb**   *nose + the dog = the dog's nose*

When feminine nouns ending in **taa marbooTa** (ة) are the *first* noun in an **iDaafa** or have a possessive ending, the **taa marbooTa** (ة) is pronounced **-at** rather than **-a**. The **taa marbooTa** is spelt as a regular **taa** (تـ) when an ending is added:

زوجة
zawja
(a) wife

زوجتي
zawjatee
my wife

زوجة أحمد
zawjat aHmad
Ahmed's wife

مدينة
madeena
(a) city

مدينتهم
madeenathum
their city

مدينة دمشق
madeenat dimashq
(the) city of Damascus

Take note of أب **ab** (*father*) and أخ **akh** (*brother*) which add an ـو **-oo** when they are the *first* word in an **iDaafa** or have a possessive ending (except **-ee**, *my*):

أبو سارة **aboo saara** *Sarah's father*   أبونا **aboona** *our father*

أخو علي **akhoo 'ali** *Ali's brother*   أخوها **akhoohaa** *her brother*

Family Tree

Make eight sentences about this family, as in the example.

زينة هي زوجة أحمد.

zayna hiya zajwat aHmad.

Zayna is Ahmed's wife.

أحمد   زينة

يوسف   سارة

Anwar's family

35

Listen to Anwar answering questions about his family.
Circle the correct names, as in the example.

سارة
زينة
صباح

سليم
محمد
عاطف

أنور
سليم
عاطف

صفوان
سمير
أحمد

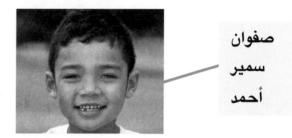

Questions and answers

Now read the questions on the right and then match them to the answers on the left
that Anwar gave, as in the example.

اسمه صفوان.	ما اسمك؟
اسمها صباح سالم.	ما اسم أمك؟
أنا من بيروت.	وأبوك، ما اسمه؟
نعم، عندي أخ.	أنت من أين؟
اسمي أنور دياب.	هل عندك أخوات؟
اسمه محمد دياب.	هل عندك إخوة؟
لا، ليس عندي أخوات.	وأخوك، ما اسمه؟

 # Language Focus

If you want to introduce someone, you can use هذا... haaтнa... for males or
هذه... haaтнihi... to introduce females:

> هذه ابنتي شادية. haaтнihi ibnatee shaadya.
> *This is my daughter, Shadya.*
>
> هذا أخي صفوان. haaтнa akhee Safwaan.
> *This is my brother, Safwaan.*

Who's this? is من هذا؟ / من هذه؟ man haaтнa?/man haaтнihi?
Remember how to say *pleased to meet you* from topic 1?:

> فرصة سعيدة. furSa sa'eeda.
> *Pleased to meet you. (literally: "happy occasion")*

So now we can put all that together in a short conversation:

> أهلا يا سمير. ahlan yaa sameer. *Hello Sameer.*
>
> أهلا يا جاين. من هذا؟ ahlan yaa jaayin. man haaтнa?
> *Hello Jane. Who's this?*
>
> هذا أخي مارك. haaтнa akhee maark. *This is my brother, Mark.*
>
> أهلا يا مارك. فرصة سعيدة. ahlan yaa maark. furSa saa'ida.
> *Hello Mark. Pleased to meet you.*
>
> فرصة سعيدة يا سمير. furSa saa'ida yaa sameer.
> *Pleased to meet you, Sameer.*

> Now introduce <u>your</u> family. Follow
> the prompts on your audio CD.

36

Key Words

واحد	waaHid	one	ستة	sitta	six
اثنان	ithnaan	two	سبعة	sab'a	seven
ثلاثة	thalaatha	three	ثمانية	thamaanya	eight
أربعة	arba'a	four	تسعة	tis'a	nine
خمسة	khamsa	five	عشرة	'ashara	ten

 ## Language Focus

Although western figures are sometimes used in the Middle East, you will also see these Arabic numerals:

0	1	2	3	4	5	6	7	8	9	10
٠	١	٢	٣	٤	٥	٦	٧	٨	٩	١٠

A peculiarity of Arabic numbers is that the figures are written *left to right*, i.e. in the opposite direction to the rest of the script:

10 = ١٠   65 = ٦٥   3947 = ٣٩٤٧

How many?

Match the numbers with the figures, as in the example.

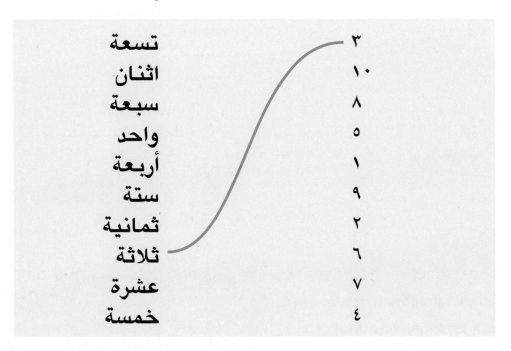

تسعة	٣
اثنان	١٠
سبعة	٨
واحد	٥
أربعة	١
ستة	٩
ثمانية	٢
ثلاثة	٦
عشرة	٧
خمسة	٤

Arabic sums

Circle the correct answer to these sums, as in the example.

عشرة تسعة ثمانية سبعة ستة خمسة (أربعة) ثلاثة اثنان واحد = ثلاثة + واحد	**1**
عشرة تسعة ثمانية سبعة ستة خمسة أربعة ثلاثة اثنان واحد = اثنان + أربعة	**2**
عشرة تسعة ثمانية سبعة ستة خمسة أربعة ثلاثة اثنان واحد = أربعة × اثنان	**3**
عشرة تسعة ثمانية سبعة ستة خمسة أربعة ثلاثة اثنان واحد = ثلاثة + خمسة	**4**
عشرة تسعة ثمانية سبعة ستة خمسة أربعة ثلاثة اثنان واحد = ثلاثة – ستة	**5**
عشرة تسعة ثمانية سبعة ستة خمسة أربعة ثلاثة اثنان واحد = ثلاثة + سبعة	**6**
عشرة تسعة ثمانية سبعة ستة خمسة أربعة ثلاثة اثنان واحد = أربعة – تسعة	**7**
عشرة تسعة ثمانية سبعة ستة خمسة أربعة ثلاثة اثنان واحد = اثنان + ثمانية	**8**
عشرة تسعة ثمانية سبعة ستة خمسة أربعة ثلاثة اثنان واحد = ثلاثة × ثلاثة	**9**
عشرة تسعة ثمانية سبعة ستة خمسة أربعة ثلاثة اثنان واحد = خمسة – ستة	**10**

Language Focus

Arabic has a special *dual* form used only for talking about two things. Instead of using
اثنان **ithnaan** (*two*) followed by a plural noun, a dual ending ان **aan** is added to the end
of the singular noun:

طفل	طفلان	ثلاثة أطفال
Tifl	**Tiflaan**	**thalaathat aTfaal**
(a) child	*two children*	*three children*

My family

Make sentences about your own family, using عندي and ليس عندي, for example:

عندي أختان. **'indee ukhtaan.** *I have two sisters.*

ليس عندي أطفال. **laysa 'indee aTfaal.** *I don't have any children.*

Look back at page 64 to remind yourself of the members of the family.

Listen and speak

Now imagine you are with some of your family looking for the station
and you meet an Arab friend.

38

Prepare carefully the information below which you will need to take part
in the conversation. Then go to your audio CD and see how you get on
introducing your family.

1 Think of two members of your family – one male and one female. For example,
your husband and your daughter; or your brother and your mother.

2 How would you introduce them and tell someone their names in Arabic?

3 How do you ask *How do I get to the station?*

4 How do you say *thank you* and *goodbye*?

You can repeat the conversation, but this time use two different members of your
family and ask how to get to the bus stop.

Bingo!

1. Cut out the small number tokens and the bingo cards on Game Card 7.

2. Find 16 buttons for each player or make 16 small blank pieces of card (to cover the squares on the bingo card).

3. Put the tokens into a bag and shake thoroughly.

4. Pull out a number token and say the number out loud in Arabic.

5. If you have that number on your card, cover the square with a button or blank piece of card. If you have more than one square with that number, you can only cover one.

6. Put the number token back in the bag and shake again.

7. Repeat steps 3–6 until you have all the squares covered on the bingo card.
   Then you can shout:
   كسبت! kasabt! (*I've won!*)

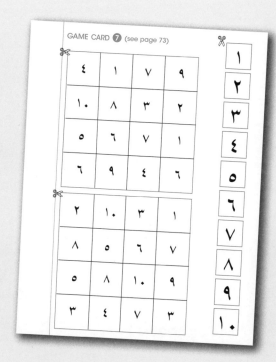

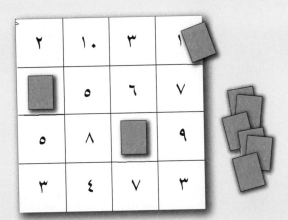

 Key Words

39

مدرس mudarris   *teacher*
(*pl.* **-oon**)

صياد Sayyaad   *fisherman*
(*pl.* **-oon**)

طالب Taalib   *student*
(*pl.* **Tullaab**)

مهندس muhandis   *engineer*
(*pl.* **-oon**)

طبيب Tabeeb   *doctor*
(*pl.* **aTibbaa'**)

محاسب muHaasib   *accountant*
(*pl.* **-oon**)

طباخ Tabbaakh   *cook/chef*
(*pl.* **-oon**)

سائق saa'iq   *driver*
(*pl.* **-oon**)

موظف muwaZZaf   *employee*
(*pl.* **-oon**)

ممثل mumaththil   *actor*
(*pl.* **-oon**)

If your occupation or those of your family aren't listed here, try to find out what they are in Arabic.

What does it mean?

Join the Arabic to the pronunciation and the English, as in the example.

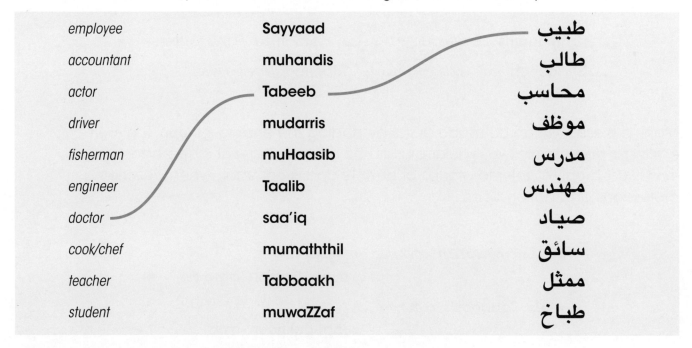

English	Pronunciation	Arabic
employee	Sayyaad	طبيب
accountant	muhandis	طالب
actor	Tabeeb	محاسب
driver	mudarris	موظف
fisherman	muHaasib	مدرس
engineer	Taalib	مهندس
doctor	saa'iq	صياد
cook/chef	mumaththil	سائق
teacher	Tabbaakh	ممثل
student	muwaZZaf	طباخ

The tools of the trade

Match the jobs to the tools of the trade, as in the example.

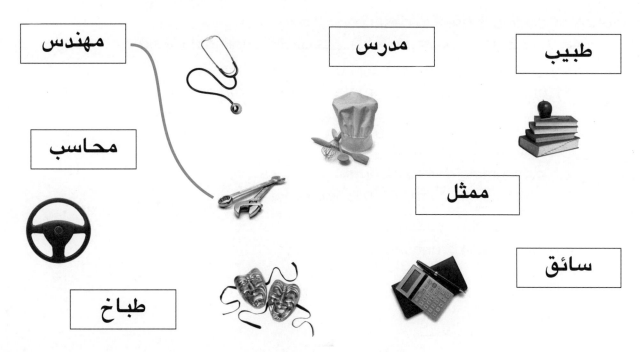

 *Language Focus*

If you want to refer to a female profession, you need to add ة -a:

مدرس mudarris *male teacher* → مدرسة mudarrisa *female teacher*

طبيب Tabeeb *male doctor* → طبيبة Tabeeba *female doctor*

Many professions can be made plural by adding the ending ون -oon. The -oon ending is one of only two regular plurals, the other being -aat (see page 40). -oon is used <u>only</u> to refer to groups of people and is common when describing professions and nationalities.

موظف muwaZZaf *employee* → موظفـون
muwaZZafoon *employees*

طباخ Tabbaakh *cook* → طباخون
Tabbaakhoon *cooks*

أمريكي amreekee *American* → أمريكيون
amreekeeoon *Americans*

The **-aat** plural ending is used to describe a group of only females:
موظفات muwaZZafaat (*female employees*), طباخات Tabbaakhaat (*female cooks*).

To ask someone about their job you can use the question ما عملك؟
maa 'amalak?, or maa 'amalik? for a female (literally *what your work?*).

ما عملك؟ أنا مدرس.
maa 'amalak? ana mudarris.
What do you (masculine) do? I'm a teacher.

ما عملك؟ أنا محاسبة.
maa 'amalik? ana muHaasiba.
What do you (feminine) do? I'm an accountant.

40

Listen and note

Listen to two people telling you about themselves and fill in the details in English on the forms below.

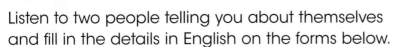

First name: ......Miryam...............................

Family name: ....

Nationality: ....

Name of spouse: ....

No. of children: ....

Occupation: ....

First name: ....

Family name: ....

Nationality: ....

Name of spouse: ....

No. of children: ....

Occupation: ....

41

Your turn to speak

Now you give same information about yourself.
Follow the prompts on your audio CD.

What's the answer?

Match the questions to the answers.

For example: **a6**

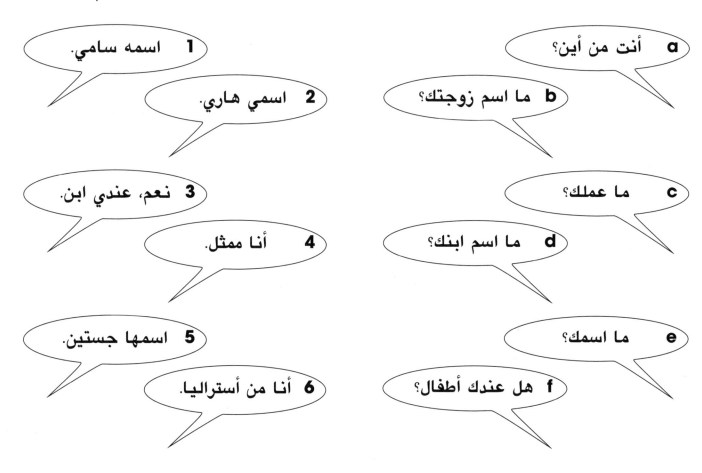

1 اسمه سامي.

2 اسمي هاري.

3 نعم، عندي ابن.

4 أنا ممثل.

5 اسمها جستين.

6 أنا من أستراليا.

a أنت من أين؟

b ما اسم زوجتك؟

c ما عملك؟

d ما اسم ابنك؟

e ما اسمك؟

f هل عندك أطفال؟

Which word?

Write the correct number of the word in the box to complete the description, as in the example.

اسمي هاري وأنا ___2___. أنا من ملبورن في ـــــــ. زوجتي جوسلين و ـــــــ ابن اسمه ـــــــ.

1 سامي		2 ممثل		
3 اسمها	4 أستراليا		5 عندنا	

 Key Words

42

مصنع maSna' (*pl.* maSaani')	factory	مكتب maktab (*pl.* makaatib)	office
مستشفى mustashfa (*pl.* -yaat)	hospital	جامعة jaami'a (*pl.* jaami'aat)	college/ university
محل maHall (*pl.* -aat)	store	شركة sharika (*pl.* -aat)	company/ business
مسرح masraH (*pl.* masaariH)	theatre		

Look back as well at the Key Words on page 54 for other places of work.

 Language Focus

To describe where you work or who you work for, you can say ...أنا أعمل في
ana **a'mal fee...** (*I work in...*):

أنا طبيب وأنا أعمل في مستشفى صغير قريب من بيتي.
ana Tabeeb wa-ana a'mal fee mustashfa Sagheer qareeb min baytee.
I'm a doctor and I work in a small hospital near my house.

أنا محاسبة وأنا أعمل في شركة كبيرة في القاهرة.
ana muHaasiba wa-ana a'mal fee sharika kabeera fil-qaahira.
I'm an accountant and I work in a large company in Cairo.

Word Square

Can you find the 8 different work places in the word square?
Write out the meaning for the words you have found.

ط	ب	م	ع	ط	مـ	ي	قـ
ر	ى	فـ	شـ	تـ	ســ	مـ	لـ
س	ب	تـ	كـ	مـ	أ	ز	ظـ
ي	جـ	يـ	م	ع	ذ	صـ	مـ
ة	ســ	ر	د	مـ	م	أ	تـ
ـة	ل	حـ	ب	كـ	ر	مـ	ضـ
ك	ذ	بـ	ا	ط	و	تـ	أ
ع	مـ	ي	ســ	ح	ر	ســ	مـ

factory _____

_____

_____

_____

_____

_____

_____

Now make sentences for each of the work places, as in the example:

أنا مهندس وأنا أعمل في مصنع.

ana muhandis wa-ana a'mal fee maSna'.

I'm an engineer and I work in a factory.

What are they saying?

Match the people with what they are saying. For example: **1d**

1   أنا أعمل في مدرسة في إنجلترا.

2   أنا أعمل في مطعم في القاهرة.

3   أنا أعمل في بنك أمريكي.

4   أنا أعمل في محل في باريس.

5   أنا أعمل في مسرح في كندا.

6   أنا أعمل في مصنع في دمشق.

a

b

c

d

e

f

43

Listen and speak

Imagine you are a chef. You're meeting someone for the
first time and they are asking you about yourself.

Prepare carefully the information below you will need to take part in the conversation.
Then go to your audio CD and see how you get on talking about yourself.

1 Your name is **Ali Al-Halabee** (علي الحلبي).

2 You're from Damascus.

3 You're a chef.

4 You work in a Lebanese restaurant in New York.

5 Your wife is a teacher in a big school.

6 You have three daughters.

Which word?

Now write the correct number of the word in the box
to complete the description, as in the example.

4 بنات	3 في	2 سوريا	1 كبيرة
8 طباخ	7 الحلبي	6 عندنا	5 مطعم

أنا علي _____ 7 من دمشق في _____ . أنا أعمل _____

مدينة نيويورك. أنا _____ في _____ لبناني هناك. زوجتي مدرسة في

مدرسة _____ قريبة من المطعم. _____ ثلاث _____ : سارة، منى وفاطمة.

Where do I work?

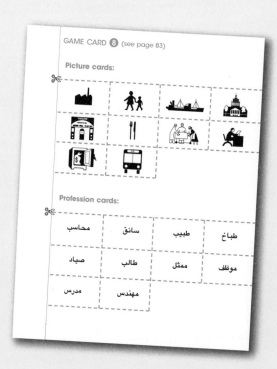

GAME CARD 8 (see page 83)

Picture cards:

Profession cards:

محاسب	سائق	طبيب	طباخ
صياد	طالب	ممثل	موظف
مدرس	مهندس		

1. Tear out the work-place picture cards and profession word cards on Game Card 8.

2. Turn the cards face down on a table, with the pictures on one end of the table and the words on the other.

3. Turn over a word card and say ... أنا ana ... (*I'm a ...*) as appropriate, not forgetting to add the feminine ending if you are female, e.g. أنا مدرس/أنا مدرسة ana mudarris/ana mudarrisa (*I'm a teacher*).

4. Then turn over a picture card. If the work-place picture matches the profession, say أنا أعمل في ... ana aʻmal fi ... (*I work in a/an ...*), e.g. أنا أعمل في مدرسة ana aʻmal fee madrasa (*I work in a school*).

مدرس

5. If you turn over a matching picture and say both sentences correctly you get to keep the cards. If you don't, you must turn the cards face down and try again.

6. The winner is the one who collects the most cards.

7. You can compete with a friend or challenge yourself against the clock.

(Review the vocabulary on pages 54, 56 and 74 before you play the game.)

Read & Speak *ARABIC*

83

This *Test Yourself* section reviews all the Arabic you have learnt in this programme. Have a go at the activities. If you find you have forgotten something, go back to the relevant topic(s) and look again at the *Key Words* and *Language Focus* panels.

May I have...?

Ask for the following, as in the example:

ممكن شاي من فضلك؟/أريد شاي من فضلك.
mumkin shaay min faDlak?/ureed shaay min faDlak.

44

Listen and check

Listen to Nour talking about herself and decide if the following sentences are true or false.

		True	False
1	Nour is Syrian.	☐	☐
2	She comes from a small town.	☐	☐
3	She's a teacher.	☐	☐
4	She works in Kuwait.	☐	☐
5	Her husband is an engineer.	☐	☐
6	She has five children.	☐	☐

Which word?

Now write the correct number of the word in the box
to complete the description of Nour, as in the example.

4 من	3 أطفال	2 في	1 مستشفى
8 نور	7 كبيرة	6 زوجي	5 أنا

اسمي ____ ⁸ . ____ من حلب، مدينة ____ في سوريا.

أنا مدرسة ____ السعودية و ____ طبيب هناك في ____

قريب ____ المدرسة. عندنا أربعة ____ : ابن وثلاث بنات.

Can you try and make up a similar description about yourself?

Read and check

Look at the picture and decide if the sentences are true or false.
Look back at topics 4–6 if you are unsure of any of the words.

False	True	
☐	☐	1 هناك بنك في الصورة.
☐	☐	2 هناك مستشفى بجانب البنك.
☐	☐	3 هناك مدرسة بجانب البنك.
☐	☐	4 هناك كلب في الشارع.
☐	☐	5 ليس هناك سيارات في الصورة.
☐	☐	6 ليس هناك طائرات في الصورة.
☐	☐	7 هناك قطة صغيرة فوق السيارة.
☐	☐	8 هناك شجر طويل وراء المدرسة.
☐	☐	9 هناك دراجة قديمة أمام المستشفى.

What does it mean?

Can you remember these words? Join the words and write the pronunciation next to the Arabic, as in the example.

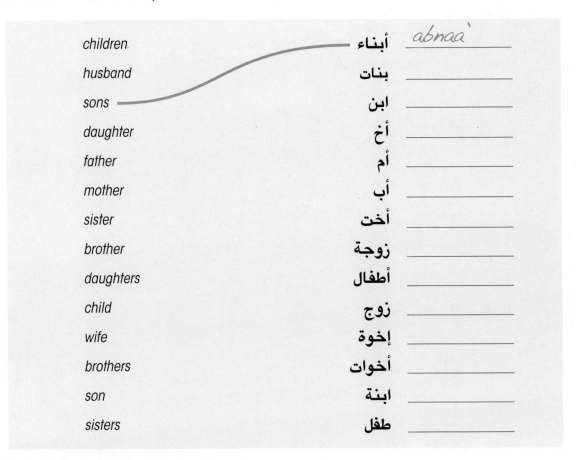

children	أبناء	*abnaa`*
husband	بنات	
sons	ابن	
daughter	أخ	
father	أم	
mother	أب	
sister	أخت	
brother	زوجة	
daughters	أطفال	
child	زوج	
wife	إخوة	
brothers	أخوات	
son	ابنة	
sisters	طفل	

How do you say it?

Now see if you can say these in Arabic, as in the example.

1 My husband is a doctor.

زوجي طبيب. **zawjee Tabeeb.**

2 I have four children.

3 His son is an engineer.

4 Sameer's mother is from Saudi.

5 My wife's name is Jocelyn.

6 Her brother is an actor.

7 I don't have any sisters.

8 I have three daughters.

At the tourist office

45

Finally, you are going to test your new Arabic conversational skills by joining in the dialogue on your audio CD.

You're going to ask for some information at a tourist information office.

To prepare, first see if you can remember these words and phrases. Write the English next to the Arabic, as in the example.

مع السلامة	goodbye
شكرا	_____
وراء	_____
على اليمين	_____
على اليسار	_____
شارع	_____
أتوبيس	_____
قريب	_____
كبير	_____
متحف	_____
أين	_____
صباح الخير	_____

Now follow the prompts on your audio CD. Don't worry if you don't manage everything the first time around. Just keep repeating it until you are fluent.

Congratulations on successfully completing this introductory *Read & Speak Arabic* programme. You have overcome the obstacle of learning an unfamiliar language and a different script. You should now have the confidence to enjoy using the Arabic you have learnt. You have also acquired a sound basis from which to expand your language skills in whichever direction you choose. Good luck!

This *Reference* section gives an overview of the Arabic script and pronunciation. You can use it to refer to as you work your way through the *Read & Speak Arabic* programme. Don't expect to take it all in from the beginning. *Read & Speak Arabic* is designed to build your confidence step by step as you progress through the topics. The details will start to fall into place gradually as you become more familiar with the Arabic script and language.

The Arabic script

The Arabic script is written from *right to left*, i.e. the opposite direction to English. The alphabet has 28 letters, no capitals, and – unlike English – words are generally spelt as they sound.

The letters in an Arabic word are "joined up" — you cannot "print" a word as you can in English. When the letters join to other letters they change their shape. The most common change is that letters lose their "tails" when joined to a following letter (on the right):

read this way ←

م + س = مس

س + م = سم

ق + ل = قل

ب + ر = بر

Because letters change their shape like this, they have an *initial*, a *medial* (middle) and a *final* form. For example, the letter ج (**jeem**) changes like this:

initial (at the beginning): جـر

medial (in the middle): فـجـل

final (at the end): هـج

A few letters, such as ه (**haa**) and ك (**kaaf**), change their shapes more radically. In addition, six letters – و (**waw**), ا (**alif**), د (**daal**), ذ (**тнaal**), ر (**raa**), and ز (**zay**) – only join to the letter before and <u>never</u> to the letter following and so hardly change shape at all.

You will find details of how the individual letters change their shape in the alphabet table on page 90.

The Arabic alphabet

The table below shows all the Arabic letters in the three positions, with the Arabic letter name, followed by the sound. Remember that this is just for reference and you shouldn't expect to take it all in at once. If you know the basic principles of how the Arabic script works, you will slowly come to recognize the individual letters.

	initial:	medial:	final:		initial:	medial:	final:		initial:	medial:	final:
alif[1] **a/u/i/aa**	١	١	١	zay **z**	ز	ز	ز	qaaf **q**	قـ	ـقـ	ق
baa **b**	بـ	ـبـ	ب	seen **s**	سـ	ـسـ	س	kaaf **k**	كـ	ـكـ	ك
taa **t**	تـ	ـتـ	ت	sheen **sh**	شـ	ـشـ	ش	laam[2] **l**	لـ	ـلـ	ل
thaa **th**	ثـ	ـثـ	ث	saad **s**	صـ	ـصـ	ص	meem **m**	مـ	ـمـ	م
jaa **j**	جـ	ـجـ	ج	Daad **D**	ضـ	ـضـ	ض	noon **n**	نـ	ـنـ	ن
Haa **H**	حـ	ـحـ	ح	Taa **T**	طـ	ـطـ	ط	haa **h**	هـ	ـهـ	ه/ة
khaa **kh**	خـ	ـخـ	خ	Zaa **Z**	ظـ	ـظـ	ظ	waaw **w/oo**	و	و	و
daal **d**	د	ـد	د	'ayn **'**	عـ	ـعـ	ع/ع	yaa **y/ee**	يـ	ـيـ	ي
THaal **TH**	ذ	ـذ	ذ	ghayn **gh**	غـ	ـغـ	غ/غ				
raa **r**	ر	ر	ر	faa **f**	فـ	ـفـ	ف				

(1) When **alif** begins a word it is usually written with a **hamza** sign, written <u>above</u> (أ) if the word starts with **a** or **u**; or <u>below</u> (إ) if the word starts with **i**. A **madda** sign is written above (آ) if the word starts with a long **aa**.

(2) Note the special combination when **alif** is written after **laam**: لا.

In written Arabic, the three short vowels (**a, i, u**) and a sign showing a letter is doubled are not normally included as part of the main script. They can be written as symbols above or below the letter: the short **a** as a dash above the letter; the short **i** as a dash below; the short **u** as a comma-shape above. The doubled letter symbol (**shadda**) can be written as a small "*w*" shape above the letter. Here are some example of Arabic words including these symbols:

كِتاب **kitaab** *book*   مَجلّة **majalla** *magazine*

شُبّاك **shubbaak** *window*   كَلب **kalb** *dog*

However, most written material omits these symbols making it important for you to be able to recognize a word without them. In this book we have not included the vowel and doubling symbols, but the pronunciation guide will show you how to say the word. You will find it more useful to be able to read the Arabic script without the symbols from the beginning as then you can recognize simple notices, advertisements and signs more easily.

Pronunciation

The pronunciation of Arabic varies depending on the region and the level of formality. We have steered a middle course, using a friendly standard pronunciation. We have avoided both colloquialisms and the finer grammatical embellishments of "high Arabic".

Many Arabic letters are pronounced in a similar way to their English equivalents. Some are less familiar. Pay special attention to these letters:

ص **(Saad)**; ض **(Daad)**; ط **(Taa)**; ظ **(Zaa)**	emphatic letters, pronounced with the tongue on the roof of the mouth rather than up against the teeth – written with a capital letter in the pronunciation to distinguish them from their non-emphatic equivalents
ح **(Haa)**	pronounced as a breathy "*h*" – written with a capital in the pronunciation to distinguish it from the regular "*h*".
خ **(khaa)**	pronounced like the "*ch*" in the Scottish "*loch*"
ع **(`ayn)**	the sound most often associated with Arabic, and the most difficult to produce: a sort of guttural "*ah*"-sound
غ **(ghayn)**	pronounced like the French throaty "*r*"
ث **(thaa)**; ذ **(THaal)**	ث **(thaa)** is a soft "*th*" as in "*thin*" and ذ **(THaal)** is a hard "*th*" as in "*that*"
ء **(hamza)**	a strange "half letter". Not really pronounced at all, but has the effect of cutting short the previous letter
ة **(taa marbooTa)**	a version of **(taa)** that only appears at the end of words and is pronounced **a** or **at**.

You will find an introduction to the sounds of Arabic on track 1 of your audio.

1

ANSWERS

Topic 1

Page 6
Check your answers with the Key Words panel on page 5.

Page 8: What are they saying?

Page 8: What do you hear?
You should have ticked boxes 2 and 5.

Page 10: What does it mean?
1d, 2f, 3e, 4a, 5b, 6c

Page 10: Which word?

الخير. __2__

أهلا. مساء __5__ .

أنا __1__ يوسف. __3__ اسمك؟

اسمي __4__ .

Page 11: What are their names?

Jane	جاين	Suzanne	سوزان
Nancy	نانسي	Tony	توني
Mark	مارك	Lucy	لوسي
Mary	ماري	Sam	سام

Page 12: In or out?
IN: Mark, Zayna, Sameer, Sam, Charles, Yoosef
OUT: Harry, Lucy, Fatima, Jane

Topic 2

Page 15: Where are the countries?

أمريكا 2   إيرلندا 3   أستراليا 8   مصر 5

العراق 7   سوريا 6   بريطانيا 4   كندا 1

Page 16: How do you say it?
Check your answers with the Key Words panel on page 14.

Page 16: Where are the cities?
دمشق في سوريا.   dimashq fee sooriya.

دبلن في إيرلندا.   dublin fee eerlanda.

لندن في بريطانيا.   lundun fee biriTaanya.

تورنتو في كندا.   torunto fee kanada.

القاهرة في مصر.   al-qaahira fee miSr.

واشنطن في أمريكا.   waashinTun fee amreeka.

نيو يورك في أمريكا.   nyoo yoork fee amreeka.

سيدني في أستراليا.   sidnee fee usturalya.

Page 17: Audio track 8
Yoosef: Cairo in Egypt; Lucy: Oxford near London; Sameer: Baghdad in Iraq; Harry: Toronto in Canada; Fatima: Damascus in Syria; Suzanne: Princeton near New York.

Page 18: Where are they from?

Page 20: Who's from where?
هو من أين؟ هو من نيو يورك في أمريكا. 1
huwa min ayna? huwa min nyoo yoork fee amreeka.

هي من أين؟ هي من القاهرة في مصر. 2
hiya min ayna? hiya min al-qaahira fee miSr.

هو من أين؟ هو من سيدني في أستراليا. 3
huwa min ayna? huwa min sidnee fee usturalya.

هي من أين؟ هي من تورنتو في كندا. 4
hiya min ayna? hiya min torunto fee kanada.

5 ‏هو من أين؟ هو من بغداد في العراق.
huwa min ayna? huwa min baghdaad fil-'iraaq.

6 ‏هو من أين؟ هو من دبلن في إيرلندا.
huwa min ayna? huwa min dublin fee eerlanda.

7 ‏هي من أين؟ هي من لندن في بريطانيا.
hiya min ayna? hiya min lundun fee biriTaanya.

8 ‏هو من أين؟ هو من دمشق في سوريا.
huwa min ayna? huwa min dimashq fee sooriya.

Page 21: Listen and Check

1 False; **2** False; **3** True; **4** True; **5** True; **6** False

Page 21: What does it mean?

I'm from Canada.	‏مساء الخير.
I'm from Egypt.	‏ما اسمك؟
My name's Louise.	‏أنا من مصر.
What's your name?	‏اسمي لويز.
Good evening.	‏أهلا.
Hello.	‏أنا من كندا.

Page 22: What does it mean?

My name's Zayna.	‏اسمي زينة.
Where's he from?	‏هو من أين؟
He's from London.	‏هو من لندن.
She's from America.	‏هي من أمريكا.

My name's Louise.	‏اسمي لويز.
I'm from Canada.	‏أنا من كندا.
Munir is from Egypt.	‏منير من مصر.
What's your name?	‏ما اسمك؟

Topic 3

Page 25

Check your answers with the Key Words panel on page 24.

Page 26: Word Square

bag, book, pen, chair, door, sofa, telephone, window

ج	ب	ش	ة	ب	ي	ق	د
ب	ا	ت	ك	و	ج	غ	ل
م	ة	ذ	ب	ك	ع	ز	ظ
ي	ج	ي	م	ل	ق	ا	ذ
ع	ت	ج	ل	س	م	ا	ت
ث	ز	ب	ك	ا	ب	ش	ض
ن	و	ف	د	ل	ت	م	و
ي	س	ر	ك	ن	ب	ا	ب

Page 26: Odd One Out

‏سمير * سوزان * (تليفزيون) * فاطمة
‏مائدة * كرسي * باب * (اسم)
‏مجلة * كتاب * قلم * (مساء)
‏مصر * (تليفون) * أمريكا * العراق
‏صباح الخير * (كنبة) * أهلا * مع السلامة

Page 28: What's this?

1e, 2b, 3f, 4c, 5a, 6d, 7h, 8g

Page 30: Who orders what?

Customer 1: coffee & falafel; **Customer 2:** tea & sandwich; **Customer 3:** tea & pancake; **Customer 4:** sandwich & cake; **Customer 5:** tea & falafel

Page 31: Unscramble the conversation

g, b, e, c, f, h, d, a

Topic 4

Page 35: What does it mean?

Check your answers with the Key Words panel on page 34.

Page 35: What can you see?

☐ كلب	☑ قطة		
☑ ستار	☑ شباك		
☑ شجر	☐ فرن		
☐ سرير	☐ باب		
☑ صورة	☐ حقيبة		
☐ ثلاجة	☐ تليفزيون		
☑ كتاب	☑ كمبيوتر		
☐ سيارة	☑ قلم		
☐ تليفون	☑ مجلة		
☑ مائدة	☑ كرسي		

Page 37: Which word?

‏1 أمام ؛ 2 تحت ؛ 3 فوق ؛ 4 على ؛ 5 بجانب ؛
‏6 تحت ؛ 7 وراء ؛ 8 في

Answers

Page 39: Where are the mice?

There are many possible sentences.

If you can, check yours with a native speaker.

Page 41: True or False?

1 True; 2 True; 3 True; 4 False; 5 True; 6 True; 7 False;
8 False; 9 False; 10 True

Topic 5

Page 44: Can you remember?

Check your answers with the Key Words panel on page 44.

Page 46: What does it mean?

قهوة صغيرة	(a) small coffee
صورة غالية	(an) expensive picture
كلب صغير	(a) small dog
كنبة جديدة	(a) new sofa
بيت صغير	(a) small house
سيارة قديمة جدا	(a) very old car
سندويتش كبير	(a) big sandwich
شجر طويل جدا	very tall trees

Page 47: Listen and check

1 False; 2 True; 3 True; 4 False; 5 True; 6 True; 7 False

Page 47: Unscramble the sentences

1 (reading the boxes left to right) c, a, b; 2 b, a, c;
3 c, a, d, b; 4 a, b, c, d

Page 50: Which word?

1 رأس ؛ 2 غريب ؛ 3 سمين ؛ 4 فم ؛ 5 ذيل ؛
6 شعر ؛ 7 جميل ؛ 8 أنف ؛ 9 رفيع ؛ 10 قبيح

Page 51: At the pet show

هذه ـ6ـ جميلة. ذيلها ـ4ـ جدا و ـ1ـ صغير وجميل.
ـ3ـ الكلب قبيح وغريب. ذيله ـ5ـ وانفه كبير ـ2ـ !

Page 52: What does it look like?

There are many possible sentences.

If you can, check yours with a native speaker.

Topic 6

Page 55: Questions and answers

Page 57: Word Square

car, boat, taxi, aeroplane, bicycle, bus, train

Page 60: Which way?

1. الحديقة من أين؟ خذ أول شارع على اليمين.
al-Hadeeqa min ayna? кнuтн awwal shaari' 'ala l-yameen.

2. محطة الأتوبيس من أين؟ على طول.
maHaTTat al-otobees min ayna? 'ala Tool.

3. الفندق من أين؟ خذ ثاني شارع على اليمين.
al-funduq min ayna? кнuтн thaanee shaari' 'ala l-yameen.

4. البنك من أين؟ خذ ثاني شارع على اليسار.
al-bank min ayna? кнuтн thaanee shaari' 'ala l-yameen.

5. المطار من أين؟ خذ القطار.
al-maTaar min ayna? кнuтн al-qiTaar.

6. المتحف من أين؟ خذ الأتوبيس.
al-matHaf min ayna? кнuтн al-otobees.

Page 61: Around town

These are model answers. Yours may vary slightly.

Karim Hotel

على طول وفندق كريم على اليمين.
'ala Tool wa funduq kareem 'ala l-yameen.

the park

على طول من هنا وبعد ذلك خذ أول شارع على اليسار. 'ala Tool min huna wa ba'da тнaalik khuтн awwal shaari' 'ala l-yasaar. al-Hadeeqa **الحديقة بجانب المدرسة.** bi-jaanib al-madrasa.

the bus station

على طول من هنا وبعد ذلك خذ أول شارع على اليسار. 'ala Tool min huna **محطة الأتوبيس على اليمين أمام المدرسة.** wa ba'da тнaalik khuтн awwal shaari' 'ala l-yasaar. maHattat al-otobees 'ala l-yameen amaam al-madrasa.

Page 62: Unscramble the conversation

e, b, c, a, g, d, f

Page 63: Game

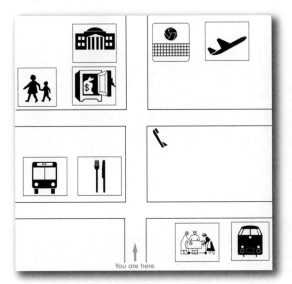

Topic 7

Page 65: What does it mean?

Check your answers with the Key Words panel on page 64.

Page 67: Family Tree

Here are some possible sentences. Yours may vary.

زينة هي أم سارة. zayna hiya umm saara.

زينة هي أم يوسف. zayna hiya umm yoosef.

أحمد هو أبو سارة. aHmad huwa aboo saara.

أحمد هو أبو يوسف. aHmad huwa aboo yoosef.

سارة هي ابنة أحمد وزينة. saara hiya ibnat aHmad wa zayna.

يوسف هو ابن أحمد وزينة. yoosef huwa ibn aHmad wa zayna.

يوسف هو أخو سارة. yoosef huwa akhoo saara.

سارة هي أخت يوسف. saara hiya ukht yoosef.

أحمد هو زوج زينة. aHmad huwa zawj zayna.

Page 68: Family Tree

Page 68: Questions and answers

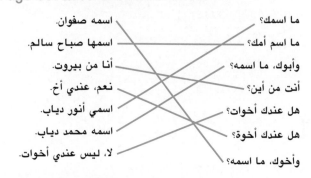

Page 71: How many?

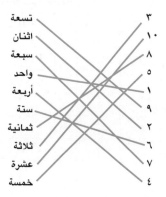

Page 71: Arabic sums

ثلاثة 5 ؛ ثمانية 4 ؛ ثمانية 3 ؛ ستة 2 ؛ أربعة 1
واحد 10 ؛ تسعة 9 ؛ عشرة 8 ؛ خمسة 7 ؛ تسعة 6

Answers

Topic 8

Page 75: What does it mean?
Check your answers with the Key Words panel on page 74.

Page 75: The tools of the trade

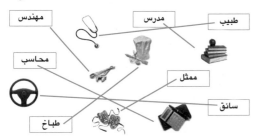

مهندس — مدرس — طبيب
محاسب — ممثل — سائق
طباخ

Page 77: Listen and note
1 *First name:* Mariam; *Family name:* al-Hajj; *Nationality:* Moroccan; *Spouse:* Mustafa; *Children:* 3; *Occupation:* doctor
2 *First name:* Salim; *Family name:* Osman; *Nationality:* Egyptian; *Spouse:* Manal; *Children:* 1; *Occupation:* chemistry teacher

Page 78: What does it mean?
a6, b5, c4, d1, e2, f3

Page 78: Which word?
اسمي هاري وأنا <u>2</u> . أنا من
ملبورن في <u>4</u> . زوجتي
<u>3</u> جوسلين و <u>5</u> ابن
اسمه <u>1</u> .

Page 80: Word Square
أنا طباخ وأنا أعمل في مطعم.
ana Tabbaakh wa-ana a'mal
fee maT'am.

أنا ممثل وأنا أعمل في مسرح.
ana mumaththil wa-ana
a'mal fee masraH.

أنا مدرس وأنا أعمل في مدرسة.
ana mudarris wa-ana a'mal
fee madrasa.

أنا صياد وأنا أعمل على مركب.
ana Sayyaad wa-ana a'mal
'ala markib.

أنا محاسب وأنا أعمل في بنك.
ana muHaasib wa-ana a'mal fee bank.

أنا موظف وأنا أعمل في مكتب.
ana muwaZZaf wa-ana a'mal fee maktab.

أنا طبيب وأنا أعمل في مستشفى.
ana Tabeeb wa-ana a'mal fee mustashfa.

Page 81: What are they saying?
1d, 2e, 3b, 4c, 5a, 6f

Page 82: Which word?
أنا علي <u>7</u> من دمشق في <u>2</u> . أنا أعمل <u>3</u>
مدينة نيويورك. أنا <u>8</u> في <u>5</u> لبناني هناك. زوجتي مدرسة في
مدرسة <u>1</u> قريبة من المطعم. <u>6</u> ثلاث <u>4</u> : سارة، منى وفاطمة.

Test Yourself

Page 84: May I have…?
Use either ممكن ... من فضلك. mumkin ... min faDlak. or
أريد ... من فضلك. ureed ... min faDlak. with the following:
١ فلافل ٢ كرسي ٣ سندويتش ٤ كولا ٥ قهوة ٦ فطيرة ٧ قلم ٨ كعكة

Page 85: Listen and check
1 True; 2 False; 3 True; 4 False; 5 False; 6 False

Page 85: Which word?
اسمي <u>8</u> . <u>5</u> من حلب، مدينة <u>7</u> في سوريا.
أنا مدرسة <u>2</u> السعودية و <u>6</u> طبيب هناك في <u>1</u>
قريب <u>4</u> المدرسة. عندنا أربعة <u>3</u> : ابن وثلاث بنات.

Page 86: Read and check
1 True; 2 True; 3 False; 4 True; 5 False; 6 True; 7 True; 8 True; 9 False

Page 87: Read and check
children أطفال aTfaal	*brother* أخ akh
husband زوج zawj	*daughters* بنات banaat
sons أبناء abnaa'	*child* طفل Tifl
daughter ابنة ibna	*wife* زوجة zawja
father أب ab	*brothers* إخوة ikhwa
mother أم umm	*son* ابن ibn
sister أخت ukht	*sisters* أخوات akhawaat

Page 87: How do you say it?
1. زوجي طبيب zawjee Tabeeb.
2. عندي أربعة أطفال 'indee arba'a aTfaal.
3. ابنه مهندس ibnuh muhandis.
4. أم سمير من السعودية umm sameer min as-sa'oodiyya.
5. اسم زوجتي جوسلين ism zawjatee "Jocelyn".
6. أخي ممثل akhee mumaththil.
7. ليس عندي أخوات laysa 'indee akhawaat.
8. عندي ثلاث بنات 'indee thalaath banaat.

Page 88: At the tourist office
أتوبيس bus	مع السلامة goodbye
قريب near	شكرا thank you
كبير big	وراء behind
متحف museum	على اليمين on the right
أين where	على اليسار on the left
صباح الخير good morning	شارع street

Name cards:

✂

سمير	يوسف	زينة	فاطمة
تشارلز	بيتر	هاري	ماري
مارك	نانسي	جاين	سام
لوسي	توني	سوزان	بيني

Sentence-build cards:

✂

؟	(أنا) اسمي	الأستاذ	صباح
.	الآنسة	شكرا	الخير
يا	اسمك	من فضلك	مساء
ما	مدام	مع سلامة	أهلا

Fatima	Zayna	Yoosef	Sameer
Mary	Harry	Peter	Charles
Sam	Jane	Nancy	Mark
Penny	Suzanne	Tony	Lucy

morning	Mr.	my name is	?
good	thank you	Miss	.
evening	please	your name	
hello	goodbye	Mrs.	what's

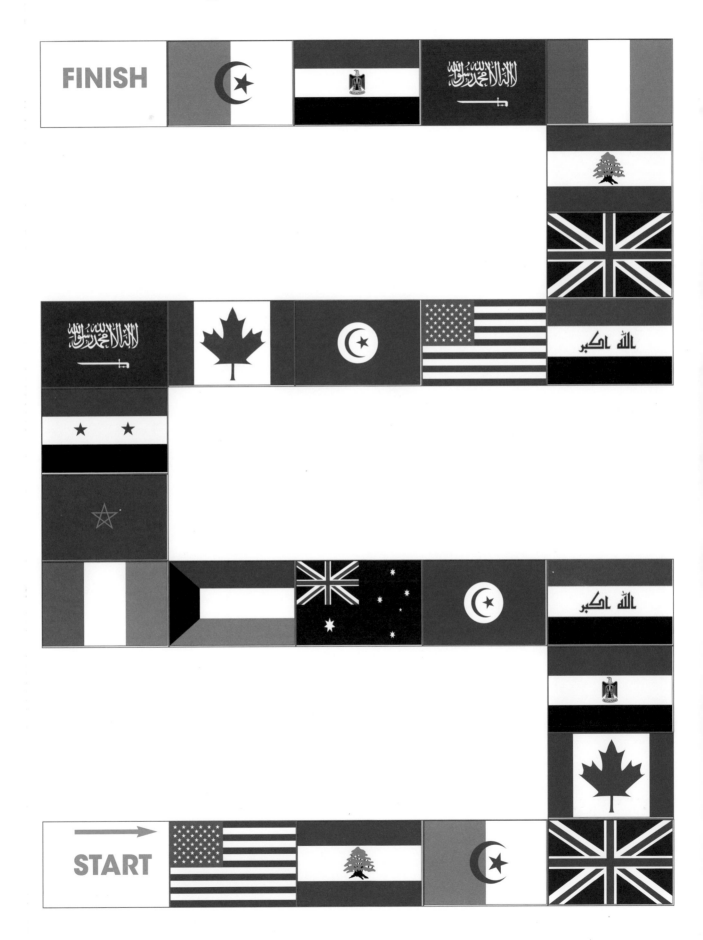

Picture cards:

Cut-out pictures (cut round small pictures)

Sentence-build cards:

في	على	تحت	فوق
تليفزيون	بجانب	وراء	أمام
.	و	هناك	ليس هناك
الغرفة	الشباك	المائدة	الكرسي
سندويتش	صورة	تليفون	السرير
قطة	كلب	فأر	كمبيوتر

above	under	on	in
in front of	behind	next to	a television
there isn't	there is	and	.
the chair	the table	the window	the room
the bed	a telephone	a picture	a sandwich
a computer	a mouse	a dog	a cat

Picture cards:

✂

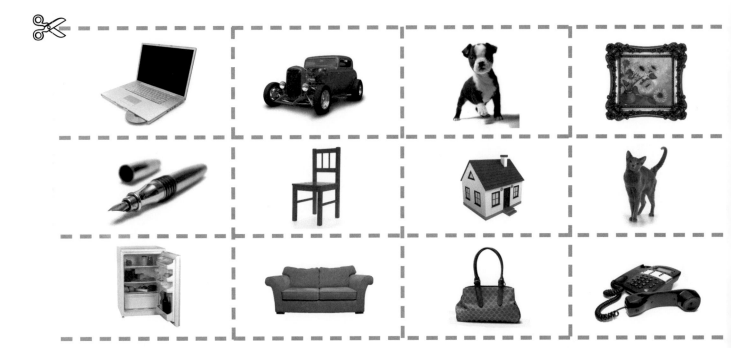

Adjective cards:

✂

غريب	قبيح	طويل	جديد
سمين	قصير	صغير	قديم
رخيص	غالٍ	كبير	جميل

Picture cards:

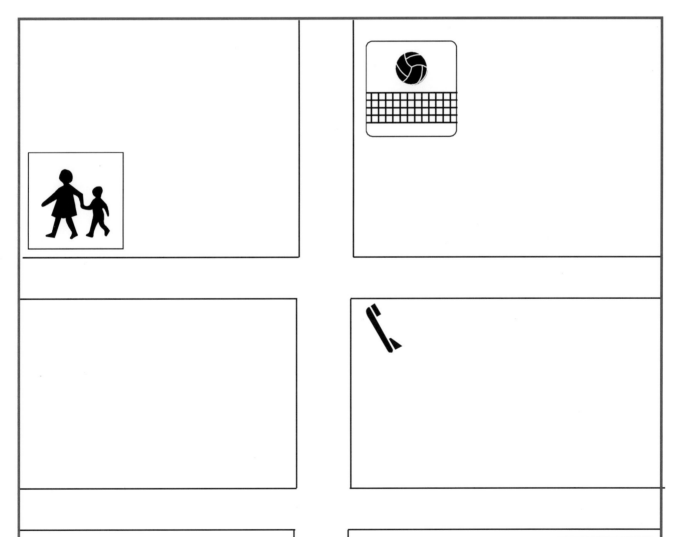

You are here

٤	١	٧	٩
١٠	٨	٣	٢
٥	٦	٧	١
٦	٩	٤	٦

٢	١٠	٣	١
٨	٥	٦	٧
٥	٨	١٠	٩
٣	٤	٧	٣

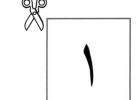

١
٢
٣
٤
٥
٦
٧
٨
٩
١٠

Picture cards:

Profession cards: